"Are you a famous man accused of sexual misconduct in the wake of the #MeToo movement? No worries. There's a new image management strategy that Andrea McDonnell brilliantly identifies as 'discursive self-cleaving,' in which celebrities like Terry Bollea, aka 'Hulk Hogan,' claim it was their public personas, not their 'real selves,' who was the violator, so they are not to blame. Powerfully argued and persuasively written, with multiple examples, McDonnell shows how discursive self-cleaving builds on and perpetuates misogyny and must be called out. This is an incredibly original and eye-opening book, truly a must-read."

Susan J. Douglas, *University of Michigan, USA.*

"In this timely book, McDonnell explores how men in power have sought to deflect stories about sexual misconduct, bringing together analyses of Hulk Hogan's sex tape, Donald Trump's locker room talk, and R. Kelly's sexual abuse of Black women and girls. Essential reading for anyone interested in celebrity, gender, and sexual norms in the US."

Karen Boyle, *University of Strathclyde, Scotland.*

Celebrity Rhetoric and Sexual Misconduct Cases

This book considers the rhetorical strategies used by celebrities and their surrogates and attorneys when faced with claims of sexual misconduct.

During the past five years, a series of public figures has claimed that their celebrity persona is distinct from their "real" self as a way of eluding allegations of sexual misconduct in the courthouse and in the court of public opinion. This book examines three case studies in which such claims were employed, namely Terry Bollea/Hulk Hogan, President Donald Trump/Reality Show Host Donald Trump, and R. Kelly/Robert Kelly, to assess the mediated and legal communicative strategies used and their potential implications. Using a technique which the author calls "discursive self-cleaving," these stars strategically craft statements on social media, in the press, and in the courtroom to create a discourse that works to shift blame away from their behavior. The book also traces the relationship between these discursive approaches and the politics of sexual violence and domestic abuse during the early months of the #MeToo movement and beyond.

Providing a richly detailed analysis of how this discourse functions and why jurors and members of the public find it convincing, this book will be of interest to students and scholars in the field of communication studies, rhetoric, media, law, and popular culture studies.

Andrea McDonnell is Associate Professor of Communication and Director of the Communication Minor at Providence College, USA.

Routledge Focus on Communication Studies

Enhancing Intercultural Communication in Organizations
Insights From Project Advisers
Edited by Roos Beerkens, Emmanuelle Le Pichon, Roselinde Supheert, Jan D. ten Thije

Communicating Aggression in a Megamedia World
Beata Sierocka

Multigenerational Communication in Organizations
Insights from the Workplace
Michael G. Strawser, Stephanie A. Smith and Bridget Rubenking

Participatory Community Inquiry in the Opioid Epidemic
A New Approach for Communities in Crisis
Craig Maier

Democracy, Populism, and Neoliberalism in Ukraine
On the Fringes of the Virtual and the Real
Olga Baysha

War, Peace and Populist Discourse in Ukraine
Olga Baysha

Energy Politics and Discourse in Canada
Probing Progressive Extractivism
Sibo Chen

Celebrity Rhetoric and Sexual Misconduct Cases
Discursive Self-Cleaving
Andrea M. McDonnell

For more information about this series, please visit: www.routledge.com

Celebrity Rhetoric and Sexual Misconduct Cases
Discursive Self-Cleaving

Andrea McDonnell

Routledge
Taylor & Francis Group

NEW YORK AND LONDON

First published 2024
by Routledge
605 Third Avenue, New York, NY 10158

and by Routledge
4 Park Square, Milton Park, Abingdon, Oxon, OX14 4RN

Routledge is an imprint of the Taylor & Francis Group, an informa business

© 2024 Andrea McDonnell

ISBN: 978-1-032-46112-0 (hbk)
ISBN: 978-1-032-46113-7 (pbk)
ISBN: 978-1-003-38013-9 (ebk)

DOI: 10.4324/9781003380139

Typeset in Times New Roman
by Apex CoVantage, LLC

Disclaimer

Although the author has made every effort to ensure that the information in this book was correct at the time of publication, the author does not assume and hereby disclaims any liability to any party for any loss, damage, or disruption caused by errors or omissions, whether such errors or omissions result from negligence, accident, or any other cause. All accusations detailed in this book are based upon credible reporting that is cited herein. The case studies contained in this book do not represent allegations by the author but rather offer analysis of allegations that have been a matter of public record in the media and, in some cases, in the courts. All persons are presumed innocent until proven guilty of a crime.

This book contains written transcripts of the following audio-visual recordings: testimony that occurred during the 2016 Bollea v. *Gawker* trial, which aired on the Law & Crime Network's YouTube Channel, a 2015 discussion between Donald Trump and Billy Bush on the set of *Access Hollywood*, which was published by *The Washington Post*, and a 2019 interview by Gayle King of R. Kelly, which aired on CBS. The dialogue contained in this book is the product of original transcriptions made by the author, which are presented here for the purpose of academic comment and scholarly criticism. The audio-visual materials from which these transcripts were generated remain the sole property of their creators.

Contents

Acknowledgments

Thank you to the entire team at Routledge, especially Alexandra de Brauw and Sean Daly, for their enthusiasm and support throughout this process.

I also wish to thank members of the Ross Priory Broadcast Talk group who generously considered the case studies contained in this book and whose feedback has been instrumental in helping me hone my thinking about media discourse. I'm especially grateful to Martin Montgomery, Michael Higgins, and Angela Smith for their conversation and friendship and for their innovative work on so many of the topics that have guided me along the way.

I appreciate the support of the Political Science Department and the School of Arts and Sciences at Providence College, and especially the Summer Scholars program, which afforded me the time and resources necessary to complete this project.

To my students, thank you for your keen observations, your resoluteness, and your willingness to point out the half-truths and untruths that you confront daily in your media world.

Thanks, always, to Paddy Scannell, my dear friend.

To my family, especially my husband Scott, I'm ever grateful.

And to all those, especially survivors of abuse and sexual violence, who have spoken out and refused to accept the status quo, we are all in your debt. Thank you.

Introduction

Discursive Self-Cleaving

Over the past decade, a growing roster of famous, wealthy, high-profile men have been accused of sexual impropriety, assault, abuse, and domestic violence. Some of these men, confronted with a potential public reckoning, have been testing out a specific line of defense, cultivating a strategic language designed to deny wrongdoing. Their discourse presents a rhetorical distinction between one's "real" self and one's celebrity image, between one's "true" thoughts and one's public expressions, essentially splitting one's identity into two (or more) parts as a means of denying statements made and actions taken in public view, on the record, or otherwise in plain sight. Faced with accusations of wrongdoing, these celebrities have taken to *discursive self-cleaving*. When famous figures strategically use their public persona as a shield, deflecting and gaslighting on social media, in the press, and in the courtroom, they, along with their surrogates and attorneys, cultivate a discourse that shifts blame away from their behavior while denying allegations of wrongdoing. Discursive self-cleaving has been, as this book will demonstrate, a largely successful image management strategy, one that has allowed those accused to persuade jurors, maintain their fanbase, and evade consequences.

Discursive self-cleaving may take multiple forms. The first and most clear-cut version occurs when an actor claims that his celebrity persona or character is distinct, even opposite, from his true self, and attributes public words or actions to his persona by way of denying accountability. Take, for example, the shock rocker Brian Warner, better known as Marilyn Manson, who has been accused of sexual assault, abuse, torture, and imprisonment by numerous women, including actress Evan Rachel Wood (Grow & Newman, 2021). Warner has denied all charges, calling them "horrible distortions of reality" on his Instagram page (Aniftos & Chan, 2023). But in 2009 he told a reporter from *Spin* magazine that he had "fantasies every day about smashing [Wood's] skull in with a sledgehammer" and released a music video depicting a Wood-lookalike being repeatedly punched (Grow & Newman, 2021). Pressed on these points, a representative for Warner claimed his comments were "obviously [part of] a theatrical rock star interview" and the promotion of a new record, "not a factual account" (Ryan, 2021).

DOI: 10.4324/9781003380139-1

A related, more complex, version of self-cleaving occurs when an actor constructs multiple, varied personas, which he activates and occupies at his convenience to adopt a range of characteristics, qualities, and/or emotions. This strategy may involve the rhetorical construction and demarcation of particular regions, circumstances, or scenarios in which certain speech and behaviors are deemed acceptable as a way of explaining or excusing the unacceptability of those words and deeds in other contexts. Here, persona play, an aspect of celebrity image management that allows stars to function as cultural symbols and to entertainingly morph in ways that suit the needs of their personal and professional ambitions, is engaged as a public relations strategy, one that coyly dodges serious allegations of abuse. We can see this type of self-cleaving on display in two recent high-profile cases involving accusations of domestic violence.

In 2016, Angelina Jolie filed for divorce, accusing then-husband Brad Pitt of choking one of their children, striking another in the face, grabbing her by the head, and pouring alcohol on them during an altercation aboard their private plane (Associated Press, 2022). As they are one of the most famous couples in Hollywood, the ensuing legal battles would find both party's teams angling for position and attempting to sway public support (Jacobs, 2022). In June 2022, Pitt gave an interview to *GQ* magazine in which he described "his dream world." The profile featured Pitt contemplating the meaning of his "authentic self," describing himself as both a "murderer" and "a lover" and showing off a tattoo that reads, "there exists a field, beyond all notions of right and wrong. I will meet you there" (Moshfegh, 2022). The article concludes, "we are like actors in a movie of our own making. . . . If we truly want to understand ourselves, we ought to take notes" (Moshfegh, 2022). This bizarre profile cast doubt on Jolie's account and attempted to paint Pitt's erratic behavior as soulful rather than menacing. In retrospect, the timing of the interview appears to have been strategic – the story came to print just weeks before the release of an FBI report whose graphic details made public and plain the extent of Pitt's drunken violence (Associated Press, 2022).

The same year the *GQ* article was published, actor Johnny Depp sued his ex-wife, Amber Heard, for defamation, claiming allegations she made that he had abused her during their marriage were untrue and malicious. Heard said that Depp, often while taking drugs and alcohol, would beat and choke her, sometimes pulling her hair so hard that he ripped chunks from her scalp (Smith, 2022). At trial, both parties testified that Depp had an abusive alter-ego, "the monster," who would emerge when he was under the influence (Honderich, 2022). Depp prevailed and was awarded $10 million in compensatory damages and $5 million in punitive damages (Rosenblatt, 2022). Subsequently, during an appearance at Cannes Film Festival, in which he debuted his first major role since the trial, Depp told reporters, "it's a very strange, funny time when everyone would love to be themselves, but they can't because they must fall in line with the person in front of them," adding, "the majority of you who have been reading for the last five or six years, with regards to me and my life – the majority of what you've read is fantastically, horrifically written fiction" (Brzeski, 2023).

While the details of these cases vary, their similarities point to a rhetorical trend. Each of these men, either directly or via surrogates, conjures the specter of the authentic, real self, while articulating other performative versions of self that straddle the public-private divide. Discursive self-cleaving activates these various personas in order to explain away abusive and violent words and behaviors and to defend one's "genuine" self. This language draws upon our awareness as media consumers that people in the spotlight are constantly engaged in strategic image management practices. Indeed, self-cleaving is a strategy only available to those who are already widely known because it rests upon a generally accepted belief that the star image is a construction, a chimera, a fiction disguised as autobiography. But while all celebrities craft a public face, what sets these men apart is their desire to maintain and rhetorically occupy various performative selves as a means of creating space for their alleged violence, even in circumstances where misogynistic and abusive behaviors are well-documented and highly public. In these ways, self-cleaving is a rhetorical strategy that urges us, as audiences, not to believe our lying eyes.

Drawing from transcripts of legal testimony, video recordings, and media interviews, this book offers three detailed case studies that showcase the features and forms of self-cleaving in action, as they have been articulated by famous men in their own words. Placing these examples in conversation with one another, we see that this rhetoric is not coincidental, nor occurring in isolation, but rather part of a broader pattern, a linguistic trend that both springs from and perpetuates existing systems of cultural, political, and symbolic power. Taken together, this book aims to highlight the common tactics and goals of self-cleaving discourse and to make its contours more evident and visible to us as media consumers, so that we may recognize it as a strategic mode of address and be wary of its intentions.

Believing #MeToo

We can imagine various scenarios in which celebrities might use self-cleaving as a defense against unflattering revelations, so it is important to note that this strategy has been most frequently deployed in response to allegations involving *sexual misconduct*, a broad and imperfect term which I use to encompass sexual assault, rape, domestic violence, and other instances involving statements and/ or actions that involve the misogynistic treatment of women and girls, as well as forms of sexual engagement that may be perceived as improper, even if consensual. Some may argue that the vagueness of the term *misconduct* is problematic because it has the potential to muddy or otherwise minimize serious crimes such as rape and battery, grouping them together with verbal statements or bad behavior that does not rise to the level of criminality. Alternately, describing an unwanted flirtation or touch as misconduct may seem overly critical, hypersensitive, or too politically correct. Yet, as Meenakshi Gigi Durham points out, "sexual violence doesn't usually happen in a clear-cut fashion only one incident or form of sexual misconduct at a time" (2022, p. 14). I argue that it is important to understand varied and multifaceted elements of misogyny and abuse in connection with one another, as interconnected factors which contribute to the normalization of violence against women, whether or not they are technically legal or licit (see Boyle, 2019, p. 65). In this book, *sexual misconduct* provides a framework for the analysis of related case studies, highlighting shared themes and impacts while acknowledging important distinctions, differences, and degrees of severity.

It is true that sexual misconduct affects victim-survivors[1] of all gender identities, yet this book specifically considers the discourse of men, that is, discourse which is constructed in response to allegations of misconduct against women. I consider this gender dynamic for three reasons. First, this is the gendered context in which I most frequently observe self-cleaving language. Second, according to the National Sexual Violence Resource Center, 81% of American women will experience some form of sexual harassment and/or assault in their lifetime (NSVRC, 2023). And finally, media depictions of, and discourse about, male misconduct towards women plays a critical role in the re-production and normalization of *rape culture*, a term developed by feminists in the 1970s, which expresses the ways in which social norms, stereotypes, and representations work to trivialize, abet, and even celebrate sexual violence (Boyle, 2019; Banet-Weiser & Higgins, 2023).

The notion that powerful and famous men use their influence to avoid consequences for the mistreatment and abuse of women is nothing new. In an interview with *Buzzfeed News*, California-based criminal defense attorney Lou Shapiro explained some of the tactics he uses to assist clients facing allegations of sexual misconduct, crafting a response that will generate public support. "We're not allow[ed] to lie and we're not allowed to present anything false," Shapiro noted, "but we are allowed to create a narrative most favorable to the client" (Blackmon, 2018). Once that framework has been agreed upon, it is dispatched by a crisis response team to secure contact with reporters and push a favorable perspective into the media. Public relations experts note that having "wiggle room for the public to believe you" is especially important for the accused (Blackmon, 2018). The chosen narrative is then taken up, shared, and echoed across social media, by both news channels and fans of the stars themselves. In this way, the industrial support of publicists, lawyers, and communication strategists works synergistically to promote a media discourse that protects the financial and personal interests of the accused and their associated beneficiaries.

Self-cleaving is one strategy used to craft such a narrative. And it is notable that self-cleaving gained traction as a tactic in the years immediately preceding and following the 2017 expansion of the #MeToo movement. Founded by activist Tarana Burke in 2006, the #MeToo movement and associated hashtag were developed with the goal of making visible and disrupting sexual violence and other systemic issues affecting marginalized people – particularly Black women and girls (metoomovement.org). Fueled by a growing outrage over the treatment of women in the entertainment industries, the workplace, and the public sphere and following a string of allegations against high-profile men, most notably producer Harvey Weinstein, and the election of Donald Trump as American president, despite the publicization of his misogynistic and abusive statements on the now-infamous *Access Hollywood* tape, the phrase went viral. Twenty-four hours after actress Alyssa Milano shared #MeToo on Twitter on October 15, 2017, more than 12 million posts had utilized the hashtag (Park, 2017). The power and prominence of #MeToo grew through the participatory outpouring of individual survivors, who shared their experiences on social media. The sheer volume of tweets, posts, likes, and comments seemed to herald a public reckoning and the beginning of a paradigm shift.

As Sarah Banet-Weiser and Kathryn Higgins write in their book, *Believability: Sexual Violence, Media, and the Politics of Doubt*, "the explosive visibility of women who accused men of harassment and assault implied a possible new redistribution away from powerful men and toward those over whom they wield social and economic power" (2023, p. 3). #MeToo allowed for individual catharsis and generated a sense of collective solidarity; it was also a rallying cry. By speaking out, victim-survivors made it clear that they were not going to sit by quietly and allow those in power to continue their abuses with impunity. But, as Karen Boyle notes in her book, *#MeToo, Weinstein, and Feminism*, what makes #MeToo distinctive is not only that women spoke out (as they have been doing for decades) "but rather the extent to which some of these stories have been widely heard" (2019, p. 5). The technological affordances of social media, combined with mainstream news coverage of the movement, allowed women's voices to be heard globally and to be treated as a cultural phenomenon. This public, collective telling required bravery on the part of participants and represented a critical first step towards the political potential of the movement (Boyle, 2019, p. 29).

Bravery, indeed, since bravery is required for any woman seeking to publicly share her experiences of sexual misconduct. Female survivors are often disadvantaged by the *credibility complex*, a term Deborah Tuerkheimer uses to describe the interlocking factors affecting vulnerable individuals, those without access to existing structures of power due to their gender, race, class position, age, and other elements of their intersectional identities (2021). Too often, these survivors are met with disbelief when they identify as victims (Tuerkheimer, 2021). Indeed, such individuals are often doubted, even when compelling evidence exists to support their claims (Durham, 2022). The credibility complex, and the way that it constantly reinscribes existing structures of power, deeply impacts the willingness and ability of victim-survivors to speak publicly about their experiences, encouraging a cycle of silence. Victims' awareness of the likelihood that they will be disbelieved is a critical factor that often prevents them from coming forward in the first place; most sexual assault is never reported through official channels (Tuerkheimer, 2021). And when victims do talk about their experiences, it is not uncommon for them to report experiencing a second victimization in which they are retraumatized from being disbelieved, blamed, or mistrusted by loved ones, friends, and institutions, which discourages them from speaking further (Durham, 2022; Tuerkheimer, 2021).

In contemporary culture, media narratives play a central role in shaping perceptions of credibility. Popular storytelling frequently traffics in sensationalism and innuendo, recycling easily accessible tropes, also known as *rape myths*, that paint victims of abuse as exaggerators, attention seekers, and gold diggers (Durham, 2022; O'Hara, 2012). Such discourse places the onus for the embodiment and maintenance of credibility on the shoulders of victims, and women who speak out are expected to appear, dress, and communicate in ways that conform to a fantastical notion of purity and sanctioned righteousness, lest their believability be undermined. In these ways, the media position victims and those whom they accuse within what Banet-Weiser and Higgins call an "economy of believability," a value-laden arena in which some actors are worthy of our belief and others are not (2023, p. 4). This is an economy deeply structured by gender and race and in which the believability of wealthy, famous, White men has long been privileged above all others (Banet-Weiser & Higgins, 2023, p. 5). Further, believability can't be "fact checked," since what is primarily at issue is not factuality but audiences' perception about who is deserving of recognition and belief and who is not (Banet-Weiser & Higgins, 2023, p. 150).

It is perhaps unsurprising, then, that media representations often function in ways that further inflate the credibility of those who already enjoy positions of power (Tuerkheimer, 2021). So while victims' believability may be diminished through a spiral of silencing, the believability of those accused may be bolstered and enhanced through cultural narratives. Tuerkheimer views these as dichotomous yet interwoven structures in a singular credibility complex, writing:

> We are primed by our culture and our law to rely on [powerful] men and take on faith their descriptions of reality. These are men whose authority is rarely questioned. And for these men, whose power augments their credibility, inflated credibility generates greater power. The credibility complex protects existing hierarchies, along with the sexual prerogatives that these hierarchies allow.
>
> (2021, pp. 60–61)

Men, especially rich, famous, and powerful men, are innately trusted, even when what they say runs counter to logic or defies evidence.

The #MeToo movement critically reimagined the positionality of victim-survivors in ways that recognized their credibility deficit and the public's tenuous perceptions of survivor truthfulness in cases of sexual misconduct. The volume of women who spoke out created a kind of shield that worked to preempt the undercutting and discounting that often renders individual women's stories unbelievable while fostering a sense of solidarity. This collective outpouring centered the lived experience, perspectives, and accounts of women in ways that challenged dominant narratives of truth, namely that rich, powerful, (mostly White) men are the people who get to tell it. To post "#MeToo" was to make a truth claim that disrupted long-standing systems of inequality, drawing public attention to, and validating, realms of unofficial and underrecognized knowledge (see Fiske, 2016). In doing so, #MeToo destabilized hegemonic narratives to, as John Fiske writes in his reflections on power, recover "some of that which is repressed as unreal," encouraging us to "reformulate the relations between the margins and the center and thus decenter the power to marginalize" (2016, p. 280).

This recentering of truth, and, with it, power, deeply unsettles those who have long been able to behave badly without fear of consequences. Public response to famous men's denials of accountability stoked women's frustrations and sharpened our desire and willingness to speak out, nudging the #MeToo tipping point. But, if we are to understand, as it is too often suggested, that the gains of #MeToo have been achieved, then why has self-cleaving rhetoric persisted, and even expanded, in recent years? I contend that the growing prominence of this discursive strategy can be understood as a form of backlash against the strides of #MeToo, a way for abusers to regain their culturally assumed position as truth tellers, even in the face of a vocal social movement.

Self-cleaving is a strategy employed by those seeking to maintain or wrest back their power from those whom they have injured. The contested terrain of sexual misconduct provides a ripe arena for testing out new discursive strategies that can be used to shore up or reclaim cultural capital (Brand, 2022). And because the media are crucial sites in which the nature of believability is constructed, enacted, and made visible (Banet-Weiser & Higgins, 2023; Boyle, 2019), they are also platforms through which famous men can re-position themselves as truth tellers, even in the face of compelling evidence to the contrary. By attending to the discursive strategies used by famous men attempting to benefit themselves in these ways, we can better understand how it is that the cycle of male entitlement, rape culture, and victim silencing persists, even, as our information and media economies tilt towards a belief in victims.

Post-Truth, Bullshit, and Gaslighting

At precisely the same moment #MeToo was making great strides in validating women's accounts, other social forces were at work disrupting the public's understanding of truth itself. Terms like *fake news* and *alternative facts* began to dominate the American political milieu. As then-president Donald Trump and his surrogates used this rhetoric to cast doubt on his opponents, these catch-phrases were taken up by followers on social media and quickly turned into trending hashtags. Thus, the rising credibility that #MeToo seemed to offer survivors was occurring alongside, and in tension with, a broader media and cultural moment in which the credibility of *any* narrative was under threat and in which the public was experiencing heightened anxiety about the nature of truth itself (Banet-Weiser & Higgins, 2023, pp. 3, 17–18).

Recall that in October 2017, when the viral #MeToo outpouring began, the American public's understanding of truth was at a breaking point. Many viewed the election of Donald Trump, whose political career was built on a flexible rela-tionship with fact and whose 2016 campaign for president had offered a master-class in scare stories, obfuscation, and bald-faced denials of evidence (Osborne, 2016), as the cause of this unraveling. To be sure, Trump was a catalyst and a spokesperson for post-truthism, but his election was as much of a symptom as a cause, a logical culmination of a series of shifts which had been taking place for decades, gradually eroding our understanding of truth. Throughout the 21st century, we have seen the growing prominence of an "anything-goes relativ-ism" in American culture (Anderson, 2017). In 2005, satiric news host Stephen Colbert coined the term *truthiness*, to refer to a flexible, personal conception of reality, rooted not in facts but in emotion and one's personal belief system. Like all effective satire, *truthiness* resonated because it reflected back to us a recognizable undercurrent, namely, a growing sense that reality was shifting, becoming less steady. Truthiness was all around us. It was in the explosion of reality television, which claimed to show people as they truly are but somehow managed to feel ridiculously scripted. It was in the rise of tabloid culture, whose blogs and weekly magazines churned out rumors and never bothered to worry if any of their predictions came to pass. And, perhaps most troublingly, truthi-ness was in a growing political skepticism aimed at all elements of the Ameri-can establishment, from doubts about George W. Bush's 2003 declaration that the military mission in Afghanistan had been accomplished to speculation that Barack Obama had not been born in the United States (McDonnell, 2021).

In a 2017 article for *The Atlantic* entitled "How America Lost Its Mind," Kurt Anderson argues that the sober, rational, empirical parts of Enlightenment thinking have, in the United States since the 1960s, gradually been supplanted by a kind of magical thinking, rooted in a vision of American exceptional-ism, in which a fascination with fantasy and possibility has overcome an inter-est in fact. "The irrational," writes Anderson, "has become respectable and often unstoppable" (2017, p. 79). And 21st-century media, as Anderson makes clear, has played a key role in this shift. Prior to the rise of the internet, indi-vidual beliefs were more difficult to popularize, especially if they challenged mainstream, accepted notions of reality. But now, fringe beliefs can circulate broadly, making it difficult to distinguish between opinion and fact. "Now," Anderson writes, "all of the fantasies look real" (2017, p. 79).

Scholars of agnotology, the study of how ignorance is culturally created, legitimized, and disseminated, pointed to a growing anti-intellectualism, mistrust in science, pseudo-medicine, and rejection of expertise as symptoms of this post-truth moment (Block, 2019). Photoshopped images, speculation, editorialization, clickbait, and tabloidization produced what Fiske calls "as if" narratives, which play upon our doubtful beliefs and draw upon popular knowledge to create "hedonistic skepticism," urging us to "have fun but not to believe a word 'they' tell you" (2016, p. 184). An era of conspiracy theories, growing antipathy to educational institutions, a politics of "alternative facts," and a digital media environment ripe with bots, filters, deep fakes, and old-fashion puffery had been building momentum (Farkas & Schou, 2020; Jacoby, 2009).

As citizens increasingly turned to free news and information, available instantaneously and in bite-sized portions, many of the presumed gatekeepers of dependable, trustworthy information saw declining audience share and shrinking budgets. Print journalism readership went into freefall (Pew, 2023). Local news resources and outlets shrunk, leading to the rise of regional news deserts and declining civic participation (LeDuc, 2020). As journalist James Ball writes in his 2017 book, *Post-Truth: How Bullshit Conquered the World*, a dwindling free press with drastically reduced budgets was being incentivized to produce less rigorous, more cost-effective stories at the expense of accountability-focused and investigative reporting. The census of newsrooms conducted by the American Society of News Editors showed a drop in the number of full-time journalists from 54,100 in 2005 to 32,900 a decade later, a drop of 40% (Ball, 2017, p. 99). Considering a longer span, in 1990 there was a journalist for every 4,490 Americans; in 2019, there was one journalist for every 14,251. We may, therefore, consider the American public of recent years to be approximately 70% less represented by journalists than we were 30 years ago (Waldman, 2021).

In this context, reporters are increasingly under pressure to produce content designed to attract audiences, and to do so with limited resources. Long, well-researched stories generated fewer clicks. Stories about a comment, Tweet, or speculation were easier and faster to produce, more lucrative, and could generate a string of reaction stories, followed by further rebuttals, denials, and commentary. And so within the contemporary media landscape, facts have become increasingly difficult to distinguish from a smorgasbord of available content which is designed to shock, amuse, entertain, and, sometimes, intentionally confuse. Few are surprised, therefore, to note that Americans' trust in journalism has declined (Pew, 2022), while speculation circulates quickly and widely (Ball, 2017).

Media scholar Jayson Harsin theorizes that the fragmentation of our media environment disrupts the notion of a universal truth in favor of what he calls *truth markets*, which cater to various beliefs, attitudes, and identities (2015, p. 4). This is especially evident on platforms where algorithms target content to users based on previously expressed interests and likes, thus generating a self-confirming echo-chamber. "Resource rich elites," Harsin writes, have exploited and encouraged "the recognition of skepticism towards cultural authorities in journalism, politics, and the academic disciplines, each with their experts. They multiply truth claims (often entertainingly tabloidesque) whose meaning, if not veracity, is not easily or quickly confirmed" (2015, p. 5). Audiences may not know where to turn for factual information, but they are consistently presented with stories that conform to their preexisting interests and opinions.

This ambiguously truthful information ecosystem is arguably more nefarious than one grounded in lies. We understand the difference between truth and lies. We know, for example, when we ourselves speak truthfully and when we intend to deceive. We are able to identify and reprimand those who are found to be liars. But in our contemporary culture, that clear dichotomy is, often, no longer apparent. "American public discourse has," as linguistic scholar Robin Lakoff writes in her study of post-truth politics, "evolved something closer to a semantic continuum or spectrum, obfuscating a clear distinction" (2017, p. 603). This softness of meaning, this lack of clarity, poses problems for anyone interested in truth to begin with. It also opens opportunities for those wishing to exploit confusion and distrust to their advantage.

To put it bluntly, ours is a media world that can easily lend itself to bullshit, the intentional construction and dissemination of narrative in which the facts of the case are deemed irrelevant by the speaker. Discursive self-cleaving is a form of bullshit. The primary goal of bullshit is certainly not to convey truth. The primary goal of bullshit is to engage the listener's imagination in a way that sways them to the bullshitters' aims, goals, or points of view. As the philosopher Harry Frankfurt writes:

> Bullshitters, although they represent themselves as being engaged simply in conveying information, are not engaged in that enterprise at all. Instead, and most essentially, they are fakers and phonies who are attempting by what they say to manipulate the opinions and the attitudes of those to whom they speak. What they care about primarily, therefore, is whether what they say is *effective* in accomplishing this manipulation.
>
> (2006, pp. 3–4)

Often, bullshitters seek to impress – to buoy themselves up or to enhance their status in others' esteem. Other times, bullshitters aim to entertain, to tell a story in a way that will spark a sense of amusement, rouse a good laugh, or provoke emotion. Bullshitters also aim to convince, to win their audience over to their side or way of seeing.

Frankfurt has written an entire book on bullshit (and another on truth), in which he makes a critical distinction. Bullshit, he argues, is not the same as lying. A lie requires that the speaker be engaged with the truth and offer a plausible explanation that defies that truth. A teller of lies "submits to objective constraints imposed by what he takes to be the truth. The liar is inescapabilty concerned with truth-values" (2005, pp. 51–52). In addition, the liar occupies a position of potential vulnerability in that he can be caught out in a lie, should evidence come to light that challenges his words. But a bullshitter does not share this risk. "A person who undertakes to bullshit," as Frankfurt writes, "has much more freedom . . . he is not constrained by the truths surrounding that point or intersecting it" (2005, p. 52). Bullshit, unlike lying, is not connected to nor concerned with truth; bullshit is indifferent to reality, and it is therefore stickier and more nefarious (Frankfurt, 2005, pp. 33–34).

Indeed, because the bullshitter does not care whether the things he says describe reality correctly, they are chosen, or invented, to suit his purpose (Frankfurt, 2005, p. 56). Once selected, the elements of the narrative may be exaggerated, heightened, or altered to provide a maximum effect on the listener. Bullshit may also involve innuendos and purposeful omissions, which intentionally allow space for the audience to interpret the speaker's message in a variety of ways. Parts of the speaker's narrative may be true, contain elements of truth, or generate a semblance of truthfulness, while other aspects may be conjured or shaped for maximum effect. "The bullshitter is faking things," as Frankfurt notes, "but this does not mean that he necessarily gets them wrong" (2005, p. 48). In addition, the bullshitter may very well believe himself to be truthful. While a bullshitter might be cynically aware of his rhetorical approach, he may also be taken in by his own act, "sincerely convinced," as the sociologist Erving Goffman writes, "that the impression of reality which he stages is the real reality" (1959, p. 17). And when this occurs, there exists no gap on the part of the speaker between word and reality. Given this presentational seamlessness, an observer would be hard-pressed to doubt the "realness" of what is offered up.

For these reasons, bullshit may appear even more real than the truth. Because it is designed to be appealing, engaging, and attractive, it may cause us less cogitative dissonance than the actual truth, it may comfort our sense of the established order, may reassure us in our own sense of the world, and it may achieve this all while being categorically divorced from reality. Lies are verifiable. They can be refuted by evidence, data, and facts. Untethered from the world of fact, bullshit nebulously floats, all the more difficult to puncture in its haze. And, as Goffman notes, the more closely a performance approximates reality, the more intense the threat, for it is that much more difficult to distinguish the phony from the real (1959).

This is an especially unsettling environment for those who have been historically marginalized and silenced. An awareness of the instability and fraughtness of truth as a concept gives us pause when arguing for the primacy of a universal truth. Yet in a socio-political and media landscape where all truth is relative, questioned, and unverifiable, those who have been historically excluded from dominant truth narratives are once again at a disadvantage because their accounts become diminished in the context of an overwhelming pool of unverifiable stories. Therefore, in a landscape where truth is completely unsettled, power replicates itself through its own ability to manipulate truth claims, drawing upon pre-existing stereotypes and biases to reaffirm its supremacy, and those who already suffer from existing credibility gaps are further disadvantaged, their authenticity doubly questioned (Banet-Weiser & Higgins, 2023, p. 143). The politics of doubt with which sexual violence is imbued is intrinsically linked to and articulated by this post-truth moment. The fact of abuse is always already contingent, unverifiable, and endemically doubtful (Banet-Weiser & Higgins, 2023, p. 20). And while media platforms can afford greater visibility for those who speak out against alleged abusers, these sites can also be spaces in which accusers are routinely cast as untrustworthy and through which hateful, doubtful commentary may proliferate. Uncertainty, as Banet-Weiser and Higgins point out, tends to "fortify (rather than disrupt) the workings of power precisely by blunting the disruptive potential of evidence even as opportunities for making and sharing evidence proliferate" (2023, p. 144). For this reason, even at the height of the #MeToo movement, and still to this day, media continue to function not primarily as sites of resistance, but as forums which produce, sustain, and conceal the machinations of abuse and violence.

In a culture where we can no longer distinguish between bullshit, lies, and truth, we find a potentially dangerous dreamland, one that threatens our grasp on reality and, in doing so, calls into question our own ability to think critically, to make informed decisions, to understand what is actually going on (Frankfurt, 2005). It's a land of distraction, excitement, and unsteadiness. Like being in a Las Vegas casino and not knowing what time it is. Like stepping off a rollercoaster ride and not being able to find the place where your foot meets the ground. These experiences thrill us when they represent a departure from the day-to-day realities of life, but when the unreality becomes the norm, when we become trapped in the dreamland, we may begin to feel insecure, unmoored, and even a bit crazy.

And this is by design. Because when we as audiences, as citizens, operate from a default position of doubt, evidence becomes less compelling, facts can be more easily weaseled away from, and those with resources can more nimbly abuse their power with impunity. It is worth pointing out that there is a term for just this kind of maneuvering when it comes to domestic violence: *gaslighting*. Gaslighting is a form of intimate partner violence that involves psychological manipulation and control, developed by the abuser by convincing a victim that her own perception of reality is untrue, even when in possession of factual evidence to the contrary. Gaslighting may involve one partner making the other feel confused or "crazy" by withholding information, claiming to forget or deny past events, or trivializing concerns.

Yet as sociologist Paige Sweet makes clear, gaslighting is not only limited to intimate or interpersonal scenarios; it can also be understood as a sociological phenomenon, rooted in existing structures of inequality, including gender, sexuality, and race (2019). When those in power persistently deny matters of public record, insist that they are correct when there is proof they are wrong, or tell us not to believe our lying eyes, they are engaging in a form of public gaslighting, designed to protect and bolster the speaker at the expense of our own trust, reliance, and confidence in our selves and our ability to know what is real (Rietdijk, 2021). These tactics are especially effective when it comes to matters involving gender because public gaslighting recalls powerful stereotypes of women as crazy, hysterical, and irrational, thereby exacerbating existing gender and sexual inequalities (Sweet, 2019, p. 852).

Sociological gaslighting may also help explain why so many perpetrators of sexual and domestic violence and abuse are, once made public, described as having been "hiding in plain sight" (Boyle, 2019, p. 78). This phrase implies that, on one level, abuses were visible, knowable, and public, while at the same time effectively concealed. Boyle contends that this type of concealment can occur because abuse is not, at the time of its occurrence, visible *as* abuse, but rather appears as some form of socially sanctioned behavior, including as entertainment (2019, p. 79). What makes an open secret so effective is that it neutralizes the moment of revelation and, with it, the opportunity for public opinion change (Banet-Weiser & Higgins, 2023, pp. 176–177). Therefore, abusers' attempts to "hide in plain sight" can be understood as a purposeful image management strategy that relies upon and reproduces the notion that sexual misconduct claims are inherently dubious.

The ability of actors to hide in plain sight, to abuse – sometimes repeatedly and in highly flagrant ways – without being revealed *as* abusers, is made possible through the work of established support networks, which protect and shield the nature and extent of the abuse from public view (Boyle, 2019; Greer & McLaughlin, 2021). These support networks may involve individual persons, including publicists, attorneys, bodyguards, and assistants, but they may also include public entities, such as the legal system, political parties, and financial institutions. Media institutions, such as television networks, broadcasting corporations, and film studios, also play critical roles; consider the role of Fox News in supporting the harassment enacted by Roger Ailes and Bill O'Reilly, the BBC in shoring up the reputation of pedophile Jimmy Savile (Greer & McLaughlin, 2021), or Miramax in bolstering the career of serial predator Harvey Weinstein (Boyle, 2019).

One of the primary ways in which media work to enable public gaslighting is through the production and large-scale dissemination of discourse about sexual misconduct. As previously noted, media representations of sex and sexual violence often re-produce narratives that normalize rape culture. A key aspect of the #MeToo movement is that its participants used established media channels, including social media and mainstream news, to push forward counternarratives, thus centering and publicizing the discourse of victim-survivors.

But the media also has the power to amplify the discourse produced by *abusers*, and when those alleged abusers are wealthy, powerful, and famous, the narratives offered up by these individuals may be even more attractive to media outlets and compelling to audiences because they involve famous figures with whom we already share a bond. Here again, the celebrity persona is a crucial factor in legitimizing the defensive discourse of famous men accused of sexual misconduct.

Image Management as Backlash

Famous figures are constantly engaged in the work of managing their public image. The efforts of entire industries, including publicists, market researchers, stylists, and dozens of others, are harnessed by those whose wealth and prestige are dependent on the maintenance of public face. But as Goffman points out in his foundational study of self-presentation (1959), we are all, us so-called ordinary folks included, in our daily lives, engaged in the work of impression management. We perform what Goffman calls *face work*, where one's face is a metaphor for one's social value and the management of one's face (i.e. image) is an important way by which we navigate our world and maintain and enhance our cultural capital (Goffman, 1967, p. 5). We adjust our performance depending on the situational context in which we find ourselves, adapting our mannerisms, our behaviors, our clothing, and, yes, our speech, to suit that context. Now this may sound rather cynical, but we do not typically think of ourselves as being phony. Indeed, Goffman does not argue that is the case, but instead that face work is a kind of consideration, a thoughtfulness which allows us to move through the world in ways that create an ease of interaction for ourselves and others (1967).

Throughout much of the 20th century, stars of radio, film, and television have worked to cultivate a coherent image, a publicly enacted "true" self, clearly defined and available to be known. This image, in its predictability and recognizability, helped endear the public to one's side, fostering parasocial engagement, wherein audiences could "get to know" the star (Horton & Wohl, 1956). Audiences, as media scholar Paddy Scannell points out, have "an implicit normative preference for immediate, spontaneous and genuine interactions," which poses a problem for "the public and performed character of broadcast interactions," which are fundamentally different from those that take place in private life (Scannell, 2007, p. 192). Public figures who failed to appear "real" would arouse in audiences "the hermeneutics of suspicion – the charges of 'trying too hard,' of fake inauthentic sincerity" (Scannell, 2007, p. 193). To be a successful celebrity meant appearing authentic.

Authenticity may be understood in two distinct yet related ways. One type of authentic realness is assigned to those persons and things which are unique, unreproducible, original; the other is afforded to those who are what they claim to be. Vast industries of fashion, beauty, styling, photography, and print media work to present celebrities as unique, aspirational, and original, but the second version of authenticity, the one that assures us that these people are who they claim to be, is far more elusive. Two key image management strategies have served as heuristics for this ephemeral type of authenticity: consistency and predictability. Public figures who present themselves, personally and through their management teams, in ways that reinforce an understandable and expected narrative of self may be understood by audiences as "real." Any change should be slow and gradual to support the perception of authenticity (Van Leeuwen, 2001). Although we, as audiences, can never really know the truth about a celebrity, as theirs is a mediated and highly constructed position, the pursuit of that "authentic" truth allows us to organize and understand our values and perceptions within our contemporary media culture (Meyers, 2009).

Authenticity is a value rooted in the model of early Hollywood, and it rests on an assumed public preference for actors to be viewed as both aspirational and approachable (Douglas & McDonnell, 2019). But, of course, celebrities have always attempted to control their public image, protect the intimate details of their lives from public view, and craft for themselves personas that can be advantageously activated in service of their popularity, careers, and financial benefits (Gamson, 1994). At times, stars swap between personas, donning various guises and embodying different roles. The pop icon Madonna, for instance, is a master of this chameleon-esque image development. We might call this persona play a form of *masking* in which one's ability to don appropriate and appropriately convincing masks works to further the value of the star, helping them to realize specific objectives, including reputational gain (Greer & McLaughlin, 2021, p. 368). Actors can wear several masks at the same time, and these may reinforce or disrupt aspects of one another, so that the celebrity is never only one thing, but a multilayered public entity (Greer & McLaughlin, 2021, p. 370).

In the 21st century, masking has become an increasingly common form of celebrity expression. Traditional media have been challenged and, in some cases, supplanted by a cacophony of new voices, platforms, and narratives. Digital technologies encourage us to see self-expression as a form of identity play, and public figures have greater control over their image than ever before, often presenting themselves directly to followers across social platforms. Celebrities like Lady Gaga and Kim Kardashian have built tremendously successful brands through the public performance of various masks, including different costumes, body types, and personality traits. Notably, this kind of malleability is not understood by contemporary audiences as a form of inauthenticity, but rather as a pleasurable feature of contemporary fame, one that allows audiences to take pleasure in anticipating and engaging these various personas (Gamson, 1994).

But while an actor may successfully don various masks, it is not true that any and all performances of self will be well-received. In other words, certain types of talk, behavior, and self-presentation are still deemed by the public to be unacceptable, regardless of one's public persona. When an actor "loses face," or their masks drop, due to a gaffe or an unintended revelation, corrective processes are initiated to save or regain face. In contemporary parlance, these are known as image restoration strategies. According to Benoit and Hanczor, image repair strategies can be organized into five broad categories: denial, evading responsibility, reducing offensiveness, corrective action, and mortification (1994). Denial may take the form of an outright refusal or may involve blame shifting to other actors. Evasion of responsibility may involve scapegoating, claiming lack of knowledge or control (defeasibility), claiming the events were accidental, or expressing a good intention designed to negate the negative outcome. Reducing offensiveness can take many forms, such as attempts at strengthening, improving, or bolstering one's persona. Or it might involve differentiation, efforts to cast other actors in a bad light to improve one's own position, or attacking one's accusers (Benoit & Hanczor, 1994). Most face saving also includes an element of corrective action – apologies or attempts at making amends – and mortification – asking or begging for forgiveness (Benoit, 1997).

Often, image repair strategies are enacted through mass media, in venues where competing versions of truth are contested and in which the credibility complex that benefits the famous, popular, and wealthy is well-established (Tuerkheimer, 2021). Indeed, the public's knowledge is structured primarily, sometimes exclusively, by media talk. Therefore, the success of the repair efforts and the truthfulness of the actor involved are determined by the impressions of the audience (Benoit & Hanczor, 1994, p. 428). The perceived sincerity of the person attempting to save face is, in this context, of the essence, as he must project an apparent belief in what he says (Goffman, 1981, p. 239). If successful in projecting sincerity, a deeply felt emotion made apparent through compelling speech, he will be perceived as truthful even if what he says is false or defies evidence (Montgomery, 2001a and b; Van Leeuwen, 2001). The danger for us, the audience, is that we may mistake the *semblance* of sincerity for reality.

When it comes to cases involving celebrity sexual misconduct, recall, here, that bullshitters and gaslighters know what they are doing. Their rhetoric is intentional. It is designed and purposeful, with a goal of persuading in mind. These individuals place their rhetorical goals above the desires, emotions, or well-being of those they seek to persuade. In the psychological literature, such tendencies are associated with a Machiavellianist personality type. Machiavellian individuals, who are more commonly males, may demonstrate a goal-oriented approach to human interaction, characterized by a lack of empathy, obsession with personal power, and desire to manipulate others to their own ends (Collinson et al., 2021). Machiavellianism is one prong in what's called *the dark triad*, a cluster of personality types that also includes narcissism and psychopathy (Paulhus & Williams, 2002). Individuals who demonstrate characteristics of the dark triad may express a sense of grandiosity, a tendency towards self-promotion, emotional coldness, duplicity, and aggressiveness

(Paulhus & Williams, 2002, p. 557). When such individuals occupy positions of prominence, they may strategically call up their public personas to conceal their actions and retain their social status (Greer & McLaughlin, 2021). Media institutions that provide platforms for the publicization of this kind of image management are critical sites of discursive power and can therefore be taken advantage of by those seeking to uphold their intended masks and bolster their untouchability (Greer & McLaughlin, 2021).

Self-cleaving rhetoric is one impression management strategy that such individuals may use to neutralize allegations that threaten their cultural capital. Because self-cleaving relies on the readiness of various publicly recognizable masks, it is a discursive strategy only available to those who already enjoy a significant level of fame and associated cultural power. When the believability of those in power is challenged, as it has been by the #MeToo movement, it is no surprise that men of status will utilize discursive strategies to protect themselves from consequence and retain their social and economic capital (Durham, 2022, p. 24). The rise of self-cleaving discourse can therefore be understood as a form of backlash against the gains of #MeToo, an expression of resistance that suggests women's claims on truth telling have "gone too far" and that men – especially wealthy and powerful men – have been rendered vulnerable to baseless accusations (Banet-Weiser & Higgins, 2023, p. 120). Only some of these men will eventually face trial, but all of them will be judged in the court of public opinion. In many ways, it is this latter court through which public judgment will be rendered. Media offer the accused fresh opportunities to cast doubt, thus re-presenting the most privileged among us as victims "precisely," as Karen Boyle puts it, "because they have the most to lose" (2019, p. 109). There's little doubt that, in a post-truth world, where the accused are transformed into victims, survivors' ability to speak the truth of their experiences is once again constrained.

Overview

This book offers an analysis of the emergence and nature of self-cleaving as a discursive strategy, engaged by famous men between 2016 and 2019. Each chapter presents the self-cleaving of one celebrity man, the context and circumstances which generated the discourse, and the role of media in shaping public understanding of that talk. At the center of each case study is one detailed interview, which forms the basis for my analysis.

This first chapter considers Terry Bollea's (aka Hulk Hogan's) testimony, and broader legal strategy, in his trial against *Gawker* media, whom Bollea sued for invasion of privacy and infliction of emotional distress upon *Gawker's* release of a video depicting him engaged in sex acts with his then-friend's wife. At trial, Bollea argued that his (not Hulk Hogan's) privacy was violated, making a distinction between his comments in public (as Hulk) and actions in private (as Terry). To make his case, Bollea and his attorneys contended that he was Hulk Hogan in every instance except when in the privacy of his own home, so that any actions taken or comments made in public could, essentially, be assigned to Hogan and denied by Bollea. Bollea won his case and was awarded a $115 million settlement. This chapter analyzes Bollea's comments at trial to illustrate his use of self-cleaving, considers why this strategy was effective in convincing jurors of his claims, and discusses the implications of this outcome.

The second chapter attends to comments made by Donald Trump during his 2015–2016 presidential campaign and throughout his time as president. Specifically, I document self-cleaving comments made by Trump and his surrogates to deny allegations of sexual misconduct, misogyny, and abuse in the lead-up to the 2016 election. The core of the chapter considers Trump's use of the phrase "locker room talk" in response to public outcry following the 2016 release of the *Access Hollywood* tape, in which he remarked upon his own proclivity to grab women by their genitalia without their consent. This chapter situates Trump's self-cleaving within the context of his political and media strategies, including the rhetoric of post-truth, fake news, and alternative facts.

The third chapter considers R. Kelly's 2019 CBS interview with Gayle King, in which the singer and (now) convicted abuser discussed the allegations of human trafficking and sexual violence made against him by numerous victim-survivors, including many who were minors at the time of the abuse. Here, I trace the ways in which Kelly used his position as a music star to occupy a dual position, characterized by inspirational and debased selves. Kelly strategically publicized this contrast to cast doubt on his accusers, many of whom were Black women and girls, whose intersectional identities and lack of media visibility rendered their accusations incredible and allowed Kelly to continue a pattern of predatory behavior. Not until the 2019 release of dream hampton's docuseries *Surviving R Kelly*, and the media attention it generated, was Kelly brought to justice in the courts. But even from prison, Kelly has continued to engage in self-cleaving discourse. This case study attends to the ways in which the effectiveness of self-cleaving practices is complicated by existing structures of inequality, power, and privilege.

The concluding chapter considers future implications for self-cleaving and offers strategies for media producers and consumers aimed at undermining the effectiveness of this rhetoric. I argue that, to hold to account those in power who seek to evade public scrutiny, we must recognize self-cleaving tactics and publicly name them. Further, media producers should refrain from characterizing sexual misconduct in fantastical terms or dubbing abusers "monsters" so as to not perpetuate the idea that a person may occupy a split persona. *Celebrity Rhetoric and Sexual Misconduct Cases* aims to provide readers with media awareness that empowers us to call out the audacity and blatant subterfuge of self-cleaving, drawing attention to its deceptive but thin veneer, revealing it as an evasive strategy and form of public gaslighting, and thereby undermining its power.

Note

1 Following Karen Boyle (2019), Meenakshi Gigi Durham (2022), and Deborah Tuerkheimer (2021), I use the terms "victim" and "survivor" interchangeably, and sometimes in concert with one another, unless suggested specifically by the context or person(s) involved, to recognize the way in which one's self-identification regarding lived experiences of abuse may include feelings of victimization or survivorship and that these may fluctuate over the course of one's experience. As Boyle writes, victimization and survival are "moving points on a continuum rather than binary and all-consuming identities" (2019, p. 15). I refrain from the exclusive use of the term "survivor," which may elide or otherwise render less visible the actions of alleged abusers. The term "victim-survivor" represents an attempt to, as Durham puts it, balance a "recognition of survivors' spirit and strength with the real pain and injury of sexual violence" (Durham, 2022, p. 13).

References

Anderson, K. (2017, September). How America lost its mind. *The Atlantic.*

Aniftos, R., & Chan, A. (2023, September 29). *A timeline of abuse allegations against Marilyn Manson.* Billboard.

Associated Press. (2022, October 5). Brad Pitt choked and hit his children, Angelina Jolie says in a court filing. *NPR.*

Ball, J. (2017). *Post-truth: How bullshit conquered the world.* Biteback Publishing.

Banet-Weiser, S., & Higgins, K. C. (2023). *Believability: Sexual violence and the politics of doubt.* Polity.

Benoit, W. L. (1997). Hugh Grant's image restoration discourse: An actor apologizes. *Communication Quarterly, 45*(3), 251–267.

Benoit, W. L., & Hanczor, R. S. (1994). The Tonya Harding controversy: An analysis of image restoration strategies. *Communication Quarterly, 42*(4), 416–433.

Blackmon, M. (2018, December 3). Here's how celebs fight back when they're accused of misconduct. *Buzzfeed News.*

Block, D. (2019). *Post-truth and political discourse.* Palgrave.

Boyle, K. (2019). *#MeToo, Weinstein and feminism.* Palgrave.

Brand, A. (2022). White masculine abjection, victimhood, and disavowal in rape culture: Reconstituting Brock Turner. *Quarterly Journal of Speech, 108*(2), 148–171.

Brzeski, P. (2023, May 17). Johnny Depp in Cannes: "I don't feel much further need for Hollywood". *The Hollywood Reporter.*

Collison, K. L., South, S., Vize, C. E., Miller, J. D., & Lynam, D. R. (2021). Exploring gender differences in Machiavellianism using a measurement invariance approach. *Journal of Personality Assessment, 103*(2), 258–266.

Douglas, S. J., & McDonnell, A. (2019). *Celebrity: A history of fame.* New York University Press.

Durham, M. G. (2022). *MeToo: The impact of rape culture in the media.* Polity.

Farkas, J., & Schou, J. (2020). *Post-truth, fake news and democracy: Mapping the politics of falsehood.* Routledge.

Fiske, J. (2016). *Power play power works* (2nd ed.). Routledge.

Frankfurt, H. (2005). *On bullshit*. Princeton University Press.

Frankfurt, H. (2006). *On truth*. Alfred A. Knopf.

Gamson, J. (1994). *Claims to fame: Celebrity in contemporary America*. University of California Press.

Goffman, E. (1959). *The presentation of self in everyday life*. Anchor Books.

Goffman, E. (1967). *Interaction ritual: Essays on face-to-face behavior*. Pantheon Books.

Goffman, E. (1981). *Forms of talk*. University of Pennsylvania Press.

Greer, C., & McLaughlin, E. (2021). The celebrity icon mask: The multi-institutional masking of Jimmy Savile. *Cultural Sociology, 15*(3), 364–385.

Grow, K., & Newman, J. (2021, November 14). Marilyn Manson: The monster hiding in plain sight. *Rolling Stone*.

Harsin, J. (2015). Regimes of post-truth, post-politics, and attention economies. *Communication, Culture, and Critique, 8*(2), 1–7.

Honderich, H. (2022, June 2). Johnny Depp trial: Ten moments that defined the Depp-Heard trial. *BBC*.

Horton, D., & Wohl, R. R. (1956). Mass communication and para-social interaction. *Psychiatry, 19*, 215–229.

Jacobs, J. (2022, October 4). Angelina Jolie details abuse allegations against Brad Pitt in countersuit. *The New York Times*.

Jacoby, S. (2009). *The age of American unreason*. Vintage Books.

Lakoff, R. (2017). The hollow man: Donald Trump, populism, and post-truth politics. *Journal of Language and Politics, 16*(4), 595–606.

LeDuc, D. (2020, June 10). *The loss of local news*. Pew Trust.

McDonnell, A. (2021). From baby bumps to border walls: Celebrity gossip magazines and the post-truth politic. In M. Conboy & S. A. Eldridge (Eds.), *Global tabloid* (pp. 153–166). Routledge.

Meyers, E. (2009). "Can you handle my truth?" Authenticity and the celebrity star image. *Journal of Popular Culture, 42*, 890–907.

Montgomery, M. (2001a). Defining "authentic talk". *Discourse Studies, 3*(4), 397–405.

Montgomery, M. (2001b). The uses of authenticity: "Speaking from experience" in a U.K. election broadcast. *The Communication Review, 4*, 447–462.

Moshfegh, O. (2022, June 22). Brad Pitt opens up about his dream world. *GQ*.

NSVRC. (2023). *Statistics*. National Sexual Violence Resource Center. Retrieved December 19, 2023, from https://www.nsvrc.org/statistics

O'Hara, S. (2012). Monsters, playboys, virgins and whores: Rape myths in the news media's coverage of sexual violence. *Language and Literature, 21*(3), 247–259.

Osborne, S. (2016, November 9). Donald Trump wins: All the lies, mistruths and scare stories he told during the US election campaign. *The Independent*.

Park, A. (24 October, 2017). #METOO reaches 85 countries with 1.7M tweets. CBS News.

Paulhus, D., & Williams, K. M. (2002). The dark triad of personality: Narcissism, Machiavellianism, and psychopathy. *Journal of Research in Personality, 36*, 556–563.

Pew Research Center. (2022, October 27). *U.S. adults under 30 now trust information from social media almost as much as from national news outlets.* Retrieved December 9, 2023, from https://www.pewresearch.org/short-reads/2022/10/27/u-s-adults-under-30-now-trust-information-from-social-media-almost-as-much-as-from-national-news-outlets/

Pew Research Center. (2023, November 10). *Newspapers fact sheet.* Retrieved December 9, 2023, from https://www.pewresearch.org/journalism/fact-sheet/newspapers/

Rietdijk, N. (2021). Post-truth politics and collective gaslighting. *Episteme,* 1–17.

Rosenblatt, K. (2022, April 21). Johnny Depp and Amber Heard defamation trial: Summary and timeline. *NBC.*

Ryan, M. (2021, February 1). He "horrifically abused me for years": Evan Rachel Wood and other women make allegations of abuse against Marilyn Manson. *Vanity Fair.*

Scannell, P. (2007). *Media and communication.* Sage.

Smith, R. (2022, May 16). The six most explosive pieces of evidence against Jonny Depp. *Newsweek.*

Sweet, P. L. (2019). The sociology of gaslighting. *American Sociological Review, 84*(5), 851–875.

Tuerkheimer, D. (2021). *Credible: Why we doubt accusers and protect abusers.* Harper Wave.

Van Leeuwen, T. (2001). What is authenticity? *Discourse Studies, 3*(4), 392–397.

Waldman, S. (2021, June 28). The journalist population. *Report for America.* https://www.reportforamerica.org/2021/06/28/the-journalist-population/

1 Hulk Hogan // Terry Bollea

Hulk Hogan is arguably the most recognizable star in the history of professional wrestling. His larger-than-life personality, shag of blonde hair, bulging muscles, and charismatic performance of an American superhero endeared him to fans and consumers throughout the 1980s and 1990s. Hogan's starring role as the face of the World Wrestling Federation (WWF) and subsequent rise, through television appearances and endorsement deals, led him to pop culture fame. Hogan was an idol, a personality, and a household name. The Hulk was an American hero, a media staple, an action figure. Terry Bollea was utterly unknown.

Terry Bollea is the real name of the man who performed for decades as the anchor wrestler for the WWF, a man who so fully embraced the character of Hulk Hogan that the two became inextricable, seemingly one and the same. The Hulk represents a stylized version of the nature of celebrity performativity more generally. Although not typically so exaggerated, it is the public personas, performances, and displays of famous figures that allow us, the audience, to feel we know and understand them. The things they say, the styles they wear, the products they buy (and sell to us), and the roles they choose to perform are all evidence that we use to construct for ourselves an idea of who these people really are. In the case of Hulk Hogan, the character was so cartoonish, so over-the-top and well-defined, that the task of deducing the clues of his personality appeared utterly simple. What you saw, it seemed, was what you got. The red-and-yellow spandex, deep tan, horseshoe mustache, and effervescent bravado were so apparent, so visible on the surface, that a deep dive was simply not necessary to get who he was. Bollea was Hogan and Hogan was the Hulk; the circle appeared unbroken.

But in 2013, Terry Bollea sued *Gawker* media for publishing a video that apparently showed him having sex with his then-friend's wife. Bollea claimed that the tape constituted an invasion of privacy; *Gawker* argued that it was newsworthy because of the wrestler's status as a public figure (Antoniou & Akrivos, 2016). At trial, Bollea argued that he, Terry, had a different expectation of privacy than his public persona, Hulk, and that he, Terry, was injured by *Gawker*'s publication of the tape.[1] On first glance, the case seemed a tawdry

DOI: 10.4324/9781003380139-2

display of celebrity scandal, a courtroom squabble over the salacious details of a sex tape. The argument made by Bollea and his legal team – that the words and actions of his public persona, a figure whose cultural influence was instantly recognizable and inextricably linked to his personal brand and wealth, were distinct from his own – seemed laughable and absurd. Yet Bollea's line of defense proved successful. He ultimately prevailed in his lawsuit against *Gawker*, and the jury awarded him a stunning $115 million in compensatory damages (Madigan & Somaiya, 2016). The ruling raised important questions about the extent to which public figures may use their fame to argue for legal protections. It also prompted a reconsideration of the ways in which powerful and famous people manage their image and whether we, the public, can make a distinction between the person and the persona, the individual and the star.

Drawing on theories of authenticity in media performance, this chapter considers features of the lawsuit by Bollea against *Gawker* media, considering the ways in which Bollea both invoked and challenged traditional notions of celebrity authenticity to win his case. It has long been assumed that to be successful and maintain public support, celebrities must appear authentic, a trait which is largely defined by consistency in self-representation and one's ability to appear "real" and therefore knowable (Higgins, 2019; Lai, 2006; Marshall, 1997; Meyers, 2009). Authenticity, in this context, also typically rests upon a perceived alignment between a star's public self (i.e. the characters one plays or products he promotes) and one's "true" self. Bollea's legal positioning breaks the narrative of authenticity by self-cleaving, explicitly arguing that his private self is distinct from his public persona. I examine the ways in which this rationale may be indicative of broader changes in the public's relationship with a contemporary celebrity and the implications of this shift.

Celebrity and the Cleaved Self

Can we, the audience, ever truly know a celebrity? Of course, we feel that we know them. We speak about them as if they are our friends, neighbors, and relatives. Sometimes we grow up with them, watch them change over time, vicariously experience their highs and lows, and develop an empathetic connection. Social media makes this knowledge feel ever more real, as details about their children and pets, their weekday routines and holiday getaways, appear on our feeds, scrolling along beside posts by college roommates, coworkers, and former acquaintances. In all these ways, we develop para-social interaction (PSI) with public figures, a one-sided engagement that occurs when we experience a sense of closeness, one that mirrors real-world relationships, with media personalities with whom we will likely never interact in a face-to-face scenario (Horton & Wohl, 1956). Most of us will only ever have a one-sided relationship with public figures. They do not know us, but we feel that we know them. PSI is established and maintained through the knowability of the public person. That is to say, in order to feel that we have a personal connection with an individual, we must first feel that they are known to us. Contemporary celebrity culture is dependent on the support of audiences, or followers, who maintain interest in and attention towards the star. Without the interest of the audience, celebrity status wanes. The cost of fame, whether in entertainment, politics, or industry, is access (Drake, 2018).

Private details about celebrities' lives are routinely leaked to the press (Ahmad & Swain, 2011). Celebrity plaintiffs have, at times, alleged that photographs taken and published without their consent constituted an invasion of privacy and succeeded in bringing lawsuits to this effect (Ahmad & Swain, 2011, p. 8). And yet those cases have done little to stem the tide of public interest in the lives of the rich and famous. In part, this is because audience response drives media sales, thus making the distribution of information about the most intriguing celebrities highly profitable. The death of Princess Diana is, perhaps, the most infamous example of a case in which public fascination with a public figure drove a media feeding frenzy, with the tabloid and paparazzi pursuit of Diana blamed for the car crash that led to her untimely death (Nordhaus, 1999). It is also because entire industries exist to make celebrities visible, to project their lives in public forums, and to understand their actions as culturally meaningful. At the same time, the stars profit from this visibility, even if they may, at times, protest.

The US Constitution does not explicitly bestow citizens a right to privacy; however, courts have recognized and upheld this right (Nordhaus, 1999). The right to privacy guards against four primary invasions: intrusion into solitude, public disclosure of private facts, depiction in a false light, and commercial exploitation of a person's name or likeness, also known as appropriation (Nordhaus, 1999). In theory, the rights of privacy apply equally to private and public persons (Franklin et al., 2001). But in practice, celebrities face greater difficulty when arguing in court for their right to privacy, since so much of their lives are lived in public (Drake, 2007; Nordhaus, 1999). Because public interest drives fame and its related industries, there exists an implicit cultural contract in which fans provide attention, interest, and financial support to celebrities in exchange for the stars' willingness to relinquish their private lives, to become accessible and known to us in every way.

The knowability of public figures has been enhanced and expanded in recent years thanks to digital and social platforms, but audiences' feelings of connection to the stars have long been a form of cultural currency. In the early decades of the 20th century, for instance, the advent of motion pictures brought performers to the silver screen, and it was audience interest in them that transformed the actors into stars. As media scholar and celebrity historian Richard deCordova (1990) writes, early actors were expected to present themselves as mirrors of their on-screen types. This conceit was supported by and benefited the studios themselves: it helped to sanitize the public perception of acting as a profession (one that had previously enjoyed a less-than-reputable implication, especially for women), it allowed for typecasting and audience recognition of actors (particularly prior to the development of sound), and it facilitated ease of promotion and image management for the studios and their public relations teams. And so early publicity surrounding key players presented little distance between the filmic representation and the actor. Shirley Temple was the spritely, talented, coy little girl off screen as well as on. Mary Pickford was America's sweetheart, the girl with the curls, and so it was (Douglas & McDonnell, 2019).

But as the technologies of sound and color brought new life and depth to the movies, these actors became known and adored by fans, who increasingly hungered for information about their idols' lives. Movie magazines communicated these details to readers, breaking down the neat narrative that actor and character were one and the same. It is this expansion of the scope of information that would be knowable about them, according to deCordova, that transformed actors from "picture personalities" into stars (1990). Once the audience could imagine and understand that the actor possessed a rich and full world outside of the motion picture, their lives came to fascinate the public imagination. And it is this knowable life – the everyday thoughts, actions, backgrounds, and desires – that has fueled the celebrity industries. The concept of celebrity, in this way, is fundamentally linked to a public knowledge about, and desire to know more of, the "real" person.

The transformation from personality to star brings with it a new quandary for those in the spotlight. How does one construct a public image? The star image, celebrity historian Richard Dyer writes, is always multilayered and intertextual, and it may consist of any or all of that which is known about that individual. Photos, appearances, studio handouts, interviews, biographies, press coverage, comments, advertisements, and the very physical being of the star all contribute to their image (1986). The "raw material" of the person is altered, crafted, and added to with the labor of hair stylists, makeup artists, photographers, publicists, and coaches for acting, dancing, and singing, dieticians, plastic surgeons, fitness trainers, and social media experts who all weigh in (Dyer, 1986, pp. 4–5). "Each element of the star is complex," Dyer notes, "and the star is all of it taken together" (1986, p. 7). The "real" person is part of this mélange, but to what degree and in what forms, the audience may never know. Media speculation about the lives of the stars creates – and benefits from – a constant tension between the concealed and the revealed. The "real" celebrity becomes a kind of Gordian knot of truth, artifice, and perception.

Celebrity is built around this dichotomy between visibility and privacy, exceptionalness and ordinariness, the performed and the spontaneous. The star must appear aspirational, desirable, exceptional, and at the same time relatable and empathetic. As Dyer writes:

> the whole media construction of stars encourages us to think in terms of "really." What is [she] really like? Which biography, which word-of-mouth story, which moment in which film discloses her as she really was? The

star phenomenon gathers these aspects of contemporary human existence together, laced up with the question of "really."

(1986, p. 2)

Indeed, much of the public's fascination with celebrity lies in the notion that, with enough information and careful detection, the "real" individual is available to us, just below the surface. Countless media industries promise to provide access to the private, the real, the star as she truly is, but all these produce is an "illusion of intimacy," a hall of mirrors, which draws us further into the construction itself (Dyer, 1986, 1991, p. 136; Gamson, 1994; Schickel, 1986).

Yet, a paradox emerges from the concept of the "real" star. As a myriad of media sources claim to provide audiences access to the "inside" "secret" knowledge of celebrities, engaged audiences quickly develop a high level of production awareness (Gamson, 1994). Those same stories that claim to give us access to the "real" star also provide us with viewing tools, strategies for deconstructing the machinations of celebrity itself. While these tools promise to enhance our interpretive expertise, they also cast doubt on the availability of the authentic self. As media scholar Joshua Gamson writes in his study of celebrity audiences' meaning-making practices, "when markers indicating authenticity – signs of lack of control, lack of premeditation, and privacy – are revealed as techniques, they can lose their intended meaning" (1994, p. 144). As we are brought "inside" the celebrity viewing schema, we are also made increasingly aware of its constructedness. In response, audiences may engage in post-modern interpretations of celebrity as artifice, becoming less concerned with whether our assessments are true and more interested in our ability to pleasurably engage the celebrity text to our own ends (1994, p. 49). This ever-expanding audience awareness has challenged the primacy of authenticity as a critical value in celebrity culture.

The notion of authenticity has been further destabilized by the diffusion of media discourse, thanks to the proliferation of digital and social media outlets, which have upended the 20th-century hierarchy of gatekeeping upon which mainstream celebrity outlets once enjoyed an influential perch. For decades, film and TV stars, musicians, and models were dependent on a small cohort of magazines, photographers, and entertainment shows, which played a pivotal role in shaping their intended narratives and maintaining their public image. Today, social media platforms and self-managed digital forums allow celebrities to share and publicize what they like, when they like, instantaneously and without third-party involvement. This direct-to-consumer model provides fans and followers with a sense that the stars are genuine in their self-expression, speaking directly "to me." But the words and images that celebrities project online, even in the seemingly spontaneous space of an Instagram story or a tweet, are often days or weeks in the planning, involving a team of stylists, photographers, editors, and market research. Celebrity culture and its associated industries are highly managed, and the details the public learn about a star are curated, edited, and carefully planned (Douglas & McDonnell, 2019). Many of these modes of self-display make hypervisible the techniques of image construction and celebs are increasingly keen to self-disclose their use of Snapchat filters, cosmetic procedures, light kits, and waist-training undergarments. Such revelations activate the discourse of "being real," while simultaneously pointing out, often in minute detail, the ways that everyone is really faking it.

These developments highlight Dyer's assertion that the rhetoric of authenticity is inherently unstable, because "yesterday's markers of sincerity and authenticity are today's signs of hype and artifice" (1991, p. 137). In some ways, this development is a positive one, in that it points to an awareness of the shortfalls of authenticity as a heuristic for trustworthiness in the public sphere. And yet it opens the door for a kind of utilitarianism of persona, a hyperpragmatism. Those who are willing to approach their public persona with a cunning eye turned not towards the ideal of authenticity but rather towards a tactical framework in which the image is a tool to be used and discarded in service of one's aims and claims to power. It is no longer the static, "true" image that is of primary value but rather the image that can be pleasurably activated by a savvy and sophisticated public. Whether or not that image "really" maps onto the sincere beliefs and authentic vision of the individual star is often a moot point. The appearance of the star is just as real as the star himself (Dyer, 1986, p. 2).

Here, it is also important to note that the star functions not only as a symbol of themselves but also as a vessel onto which culture projects its norms and values, its hopes and fears (Dyer, 1986). Thus, the meaning of a celebrity is always situated within a historic and socio-political context. How we, as audiences, read into and interpret the star sign is, similarly, a reflection of our selves within a contextual moment. Our willingness, perhaps even desire, to read celebrity as a fluid and unstable text, to engage what Gamson calls "believing games," in which "the pleasurable freedom of celebrity gossip is built precisely on its freedom from but resemblance to truth" (1994, p. 177), reveals something critical about this moment in the 21st century. Our rejection of authenticity as a primary value, our eagerness to accept stars who engage a utilitarian approach to identity formation, and the pleasure we take in cultivating our own viewing tools to dissect and discern the meanings and values of celebrity are indicative of a post-truth media environment.

Kayfabe and the Hulk

Post-truth is a concept often pegged to politics, generally, and, in an American context, to the election of Donald Trump to the office of president (more on that in the next chapter). But the popular culture, and media culture in particular, had been sowing seeds of doubt long before Trump fashioned himself as the Republican nominee. During the early 2000s, reality television shows, celebrity magazines, and gossip blogs, like Perez Hilton and Lainey Gossip, amassed cultural clout and financial viability by trading in rumor, speculation, and innuendo (McDonnell, 2021). Still, long before *TMZ* or *Us Weekly* became household names, there was professional wrestling.

As an entertainment spectacle with a wide-ranging appeal, the history of professional wrestling dates back centuries (Beekman, 2006). During the Depression era, fights were shown in cinemas and the morality plays they performed, with the good guy bound to persevere over the ne'er-do-well, were well-adapted to the format of motion pictures (Beekman, 2006, p. 66). But it was the advent of television that allowed broadcasters to beam matches into the American living room, resulting in an explosion of wrestling's popularity during the 1950s. By the 1980s, the genre benefited from the enhanced viewer choice that accompanied the advent of cable, and much-anticipated matches contributed to the rise of pay-per-view programming (Beekman, 2006, p. ix). The forms and features of professional wrestling in the late 20th century can therefore be understood as both drivers and beneficiaries of advancements in media technologies (Beekman, 2006).

The world of professional wrestling has its own structures, language, and pleasures. Roland Barthes calls wrestling "a spectacle of excess," and its mixture of sport and soap opera revels in a campy display of costuming, choreography, rivalry, and athleticism (Barthes, 1972, p. 15; Laine, 2018). In some ways, wrestling draws inspiration from the exaggerated forms of Kabuki, or Italian opera, wherein emotional displays are heightened to evoke strong feelings from the audience, and wherein the visual and the physical replace language as the primary communicative tools. This has led some to theorize that wrestling can be best understood not as a sport but as theater (Barthes, 1972; O'Brien, 2020). Wrestling has been criticized for being unconvincingly brash and for lacking the merit of real sports (Laine, 2018, p. 82). But for fans of the genre, that matters not. For those who understand its contours, professional wrestling functions as a compelling narrative arena, suffused with meaning, excitement, and personalities. To enter this arena, and to pleasurably engage it, one must abandon preconceived conceptions of taste – and of reality itself.

The question of the real and the fake is at the heart of professional wrestling. Outside of the ring, fakeness is considered a flaw, a moral lack, and the thing that distinguishes professional wrestling from "real" sports (Mazer, 2005, p. 67). But these assumptions are cast aside in the realm of wrestling, and it is the fake that binds fans to wrestlers and to other fans, while also pleasurably eschewing the academic and cultural authority of the real (Mazer, 2005, p. 68). Audiences who often engage with the genre over extended periods are highly aware of its constructions and conceits. Like Gamson's post-modern celebrity followers, wrestling fans do not understand fabrications to be problems but see them as opportunities to activate the play in service of their fandom. If the fight is fixed, so be it. If the punch is exaggerated, if the body slam is staged, these are not problems to be criticized but opportunities for "imaginative empowerment" and heightened personal enjoyment (Barthes, 1972; Mazer, 2005, p. 79). As Sharon Mazer writes in her study of the genre,

> the interplay between the real and the fake is what generates much of the heat in wrestling. The pleasure for wrestlers and spectators alike may be found in the expressive tension between the spontaneous and the rehearsed, in the anticipation of, and acute desire for, the moment when the real breaks through the pretended.
>
> (2005, p. 68)

The tension between appearance and reality keeps fans engaged in a constant believing game, one that mirrors those played by fans of actors and pop stars.

Professional wrestling even has a specific word that describes the relationship between audiences and the real: *kayfabe*. Kayfabe refers to the characters, ongoing rivalries, narratives, rules, and structures of the wrestling world (Laine, 2018). It is the reality that wrestling creates for itself, on its own terms and in its own space. It is the presentation of the wrestling world as absolutely real, sincere, and authentic, and without a hint of performance or irony, when it is, of course, all an act (O'Brien, 2020). The term – and wrestling itself – has roots in the history of the carnival, dating back as far as the 1800s, and it points to a century's worth of viewers' attempts to see behind the curtain of performance (Chard & Litherland, 2019; Laine, 2018, p. 90). Matches were an attraction at many carnival shows, and these were often fixed. The performers were in on the scheme, but the audience was not. Workers had to protect the business secrets to ensure a successful performance. These secrets became known as *kayfabe* (Beekman, 2006, p. 40). From an audience perspective, kayfabe also describes the feeling of knowingness, when we are aware we are being deceived but play along, because the acceptance of the performance offers pleasure. In this way, kayfabe can be understood as a form of both cynicism and hope, wherein perceived falseness is taken for granted but also holds potential for malleability and play (Laine, 2018, pp. 90, 93).

Kayfabe defines the world of wrestling in its entirety, but it also applies to the personas of its stars, which is generated by their construction and maintenance of character both within and outside the ring (Chard & Litherland, 2019; O'Brien, 2020). We see this clearly in the persona of Hulk Hogan, who solidified himself as a presence in the world of the WWF and throughout popular culture during the 1980s and 1990s (Beekman, 2006). Known as an American superhero, the Hulk embodied a vision of masculinity rooted in virility, exuberant confidence, strength, and patriotism. His *True American* theme song featured these lyrics: "I am a real American. Fight for the rights of every man. I am a real American. Fight for what's right! Fight for your life!" His matches often saw him pairing off against wrestlers designed to embody foreign threats;

during a 1985 match against a Soviet character, Nikolai Volkoff, Hulk Hogan headbutted the flag of the Soviet Union, physically expressing his symbolic status as American defender (Magee, 2017). As his following grew, Hulk Hogan's appeal to his "hulkamaniac" fans began to extend outside the ring, as he appeared in commercials and cartoons and sold his own line of children's vitamins. All these endeavors helped turn the Hulk into a transmedia star, enhancing his personal celebrity and solidifying his image in the popular imagination (Chard & Litherland, 2019).

While these appearances saw Hulk Hogan take center stage, the man behind the mustache rarely came into view. The individual performing as Hulk, whose real name was Terry Bollea, was barely known or asked after. Through the Hulk, the conventions of kayfabe blurred out from the world of wrestling and into the realm of mainstream media and pop culture. So deeply was Bollea's image tied to that of Hogan's that his inability to shake off these established character conventions was a primary reason cited for his failure to break out as a Hollywood film star – Bollea couldn't believably play other characters because he was always *already* in character as Hulk (Chard & Litherland, 2019, p. 43). Throughout his career, the audience's understanding of Bollea was, therefore, not dependent on a perceived split between star and image, in which the "real" person existed just out of view, but on the idea that the persona and the person were one and the same (Chard & Litherland, 2019).

Indeed, in wrestling, there is no distinction between the wrestler and the character; they function as a single entity with no clear division (O'Brien, 2020). Performers exist in the totality of the wrestling world, without ever indicating that they are enacting a fiction (O'Brien, 2020). These characters, like the genre in which they perform, are larger-than-life exaggerations who dramatically realize the feelings, values, and aspirations of the audience, and of the culture within which they exist. As Henry Jenkins writes, wrestlers operate "within a world of absolutes . . . and project their emotions from every inch of their bodies" (2001, p. 49). They often speak directly to camera, using dramatic metaphors and heightened language to further enhance their personas (Jenkins, 2005; O'Brien, 2020). The drama of wrestling emerges from the emotional and physical conflict between characters who embody powerful concepts such as heroism and evil, justice and mayhem, power and weakness, nationalism and foreignness; their ongoing rivalries express deep-seated tensions within existing social and moral orders (Jenkins, 2005). And because rivals are often cast as doppelgangers, "similar yet morally opposite figures," matches are fought on a narrow terrain, where righteousness is tenuous and always at risk of succumbing (Jenkins, 2005, p. 43; O'Brien, 2020). Here, there is no gray area, no ambivalence, no question about who is right, who is deserving, or whom the audience should root for (O'Brien, 2020).

In this way, kayfabe both relies upon and fosters a melodramatic realm in which everything is obvious, on display, and clear at the surface at all times. The spectacle of the melodramatic allows for intense audience participation – the shouts and boos, cheers and hisses that the audience offers up are reactions not only, or even primarily, to the physicality of the fights but to the emotional and moral contests on display (Jenkins, 2005). Critically, melodrama is not a performative mode that is generally associated with or made available for enjoyment by male audiences. Genres which we tend to consider melodramatic – romance novels, talk shows, and soap operas – are often assumed to be for and about women. What is critically different about wrestling, as Jenkins makes clear, is that it is a *masculine melodrama*, which foregrounds the physical strength and muscular prowess of the male body as a site of moral authority and rightness (2005, p. 41). Visible, physical displays of strength are the terrain on which our heroes fight, while villains use cunning, subterfuge, and deception to compensate for their bodily lack. "Bad guys," Jenkins writes, "cheat to win. They manipulate the system and step outside the rules" (2001, p. 42). Justice is restored through the physical might of the male body. The centering of masculine melodrama within the competition allows for socially acceptable male homosocial bonding and displays of emotion that are often frowned upon in gendered cultural contexts.

Indeed, professional wrestling is an arena that celebrates and makes visible a theatrical performance of hypermasculinity. Hypermasculinity is a gendered expression characterized by machismo and the belief that violence is manly and danger is exciting for "real men" (Mosher & Sirkin, 1984). This exaggerated version of masculinity is performed in ways that express aggression, self-assurance, and over-the-top ego. Linguistically, hypermasculinity may manifest as communicative withdrawal, silence or reluctance to speak (Ben-Zeev et al., 2012), but in the world of wrestling, it is more often performed through bombast, the expression of excessive emotion through violent, sexualized, unapologetic, or otherwise aggressive speech (Darnell & Wilson, 2006). In the wrestling arena, hypermasculinity functions not only as a mode of aspirational gender performance but also as a form of melodrama. Wrestling makes plain and obvious the gendered stereotypes upon which hegemonic norms of masculinity rest and then activates the performance of that masculinity as a way of generating pleasure.

Taken together, the masculine melodrama of professional wrestling provides audiences – especially male audiences – with a cathartic release, one that emerges from the spectator's ability to simultaneously observe, enjoy, and vicariously experience heightened masculinity *and* heightened emotional engagement. These also reinforce the rationale of kayfabe, as masculine emotion drives the moral order of this world. In her study of soap opera viewing, Ien Ang links this catharsis to the concept of "the melodramatic imagination" and writes that experiences which activate this imagination play an important role in making modern life feel valuable and in affirming a sense of meaning and order.

The melodramatic imagination is . . . the expression of a refusal, or inability, to accept insignificant everyday life as banal and meaningless, and is born of a vague, inarticulate dissatisfaction with existence here and now. . . . There are no words for the ordinary pain of living of ordinary people . . . for the vague sense of loss, except in half-ironic, half-resigned phrases such as: "You win some, you lose some." By making that ordinariness something special and meaningful in the imagination, that sense of loss can – at least for a time – be removed. . . . In a life in which every imminent meaning is constantly questioned and in which traditions no longer have a firm hold, a need exists for reassurance that life can in fact have meaning and therefore life is worth the trouble, in spite of all appearances to the contrary.

(1989, pp. 79–80)

Much like soap opera, the heightened world of professional wrestling sweeps away the dullness of the everyday, replacing it with a world of predictability, clarity, and feeling. Vagueness is cast out by certainty. Emotional restraint is overshadowed by emotional excess. Factual uncertainty matters not in the face of visceral knowledge. Neither normative assumptions about American masculinity nor popular media targeted to them typically afford men the opportunity to engage in this kind of melodramatic catharsis. Professional wrestling does precisely that, and it does so by leaving the complexities of reality far outside the arena (Jenkins, 2005).

Bollea on the Stand

But what happens when a person so steeped in kayfabe that the line between self and character is so difficult to distinguish as to be functionally unidentifiable exits the ring? What happens if he then walks up the steps of a courthouse and takes the stand? What ensues is a collision of artifice and truth, a bizarre and, at times, unbelievable trial which Leslie Savan, media critic for *The Nation*, has called "a cartoony explosion" (Knappenberger, 2017). And when it's over, we, the public, are confronted with the aftermath, clawing through the debris for meaning, searching for a stable vantage point from which to understand what is, in fact, real.

In 2013, Terry Bollea sued the popular online blog *Gawker* over its release of portions of a video in which Bollea appeared to have sexual relations with Heather Clem, a woman who was, at the time, married to radio personality and friend of Bollea, Todd Alan Clem (aka Bubba the Love Sponge). *The New York Times* would describe the ensuing legal contest as "one of the more surreal first amendment trials in American history" (Somaiya, 2016) and *The Atlantic* dubbed it "one of the most consequential lawsuits in the history of modern American media" (Thompson, 2018). During the trial, heard in March 2016 in Pinellas County Court in the state of Florida, Bollea claimed that the publication of the tape without his consent constituted an invasion of privacy and resulted in the infliction of emotional distress. *Gawker* argued that the video was newsworthy and that an imposition of legal limits on its editorial decision-making would constitute an infringement on freedom of the press and a violation of the publication's First Amendment rights. The US Constitution protects the media's ability to publish legitimate news stories, even those whose content might be deemed objectionable. *Gawker's* position was that the information it published was both truthful and newsworthy, given the claimant's celebrity status and the fact that media reports had, at the time of its release of the tape, already published details of its existence and nature (Antoniou & Akrivos, 2016). At the core of the trial were questions about whether the release of a salacious sex tape was newsworthy under Florida law and, if so, "whether it met a threshold of newsworthiness high enough to override the claimant's right to privacy" (Antoniou & Akrivos, 2016).

I pause, here, to situate Bollea's case within the broader concept of sexual misconduct that this book considers. Heather Cole (then Clem) never alleged that her sexual encounter with Bollea was anything other than consensual. Still, in a deposition, Cole testified that she had sex with numerous men during her relationship with her then-husband and that her husband chose the persons with whom she would have sex (Marsh, 2016). Cole also testified that she was not aware that her encounter with Bollea was being recorded and that when her then-husband showed her a videotape of her and Bollea engaged in sex, she was "very upset" because she had "no idea" that she was going to be – or had been – filmed (Marsh, 2016; Patterson, 2016). For his part, Bollea's account of whether he had prior knowledge that the sexual encounter was being filmed has, at times, appeared contradictory or confused. He had said that he did not watch the video when he learned of its existence, but in 2012 media interviews, he stated that he had asked Bubba Clem if he was being filmed (CBS/AP, 2016). So although this case does not contain allegations that the sexual acts were non-consensual or violent, the possibility that Cole was recorded without her consent – having sex with a man at her husband's request – while Bollea may have been aware of this fact does introduce the possibility that the overall encounter was non-consensual. Minimally, Cole's testimony about the emotional damage she experienced upon learning of the recording's existence demonstrates that she was harmed by this apparently non-consensual aspect of the encounter.

A key issue at trial was whether Bollea, who had been a public figure for decades, could claim a reasonable expectation of privacy, particularly regarding the publication of a portion of a sex tape whose contents, evidence would show, he had publicly discussed during prior media appearances. Legal precedent suggests that an individual's willingness to voluntarily subject oneself to the public spotlight can influence the court's evaluation of the newsworthiness of such a publication (Antoniou & Akrivos, 2016). Further, the US Supreme Court held in *Bartnicki v Copper* (2001) that one of the costs of engagement in public affairs is "an attendant loss of privacy." Still, while courts are more likely to find that information about public persons is newsworthy, the involvement of a celebrity does not necessarily mean that the media are entitled to publicize every detail about the celebrity's life (Antoniou & Akrivos, 2016, p. 7). So the question remained: Did *Gawker* have the right to publish the tape, or had Bollea's right to privacy been violated?

To argue the latter, Bollea's attorneys faced a challenge of public record. Their client had sought the spotlight, inviting attention towards supposedly private aspects of his life, including his body, sexuality, and marriage in television and radio appearances, and in his own reality television show, *Hogan Knows Best* (VH1, 2005–2007). Indeed, *Gawker*'s attorneys argued that Bollea's past media appearances were indicative of a man who was willing, even eager, to reveal his most personal affairs in public venues. A reasonable juror may wonder why a man allegedly seeking privacy would publish a memoir in which he discussed a love affair or appear in a reality TV scene while sitting on a toilet, as Bollea had done (Madigan, 2016). One might question whether these and similar public displays were at odds with his claim that he had been damaged due to *Gawker*'s reporting.

In an effort to counter this potential credibility gap, Bollea and his attorneys engaged in discursive self-cleaving, drawing a distinction between Terry Bollea, the private person, and Hulk Hogan, the public character, and claiming rights to privacy as they apply to the former. Throughout the trial, the resulting line of questioning was framed, as one writer put it in *The Hollywood Reporter*, "as if [Bollea] suffers from a personality disorder" (Gardner, 2016). On the one hand, the jury was told, was Terry Bollea, a shy, unassuming 62-year-old man who claimed to have difficulty making friends, and on the other was Hulk Hogan, an exuberant, outgoing wrestling champion with a long record of over-the-top antics (Somaiya, 2016). To protect his legal interest, Bollea offered up the character of Hulk Hogan as a guise, suggesting that the Hulk's image was a work of fiction, unrooted from the reality of his daily life (Somaiya, 2016).

Bollea testified that *Gawker*'s unsanctioned release of the sex tape left him "shellshocked" and that, as a result, he went into "Hulk Hogan mode" to deal with the ensuing media attention (Winer, 2016). When asked by *Gawker*'s attorney, Michael Sullivan, about whether he had told Howard Stern to respect his privacy, when discussing his sex life on Stern's radio show, Bollea replied, "No sir. I didn't want to bring Terry Bollea the man and separate the man from the character" (ABC News, 2016; Gardner, 2016). Bollea claimed that, because this media appearance was a "character-driven" interview based on his wrestler persona, he did not wish to express his true feelings, stating, "I was on an entertainment show, and I had to be an entertainer, so I just kept going" (Madigan, 2016). Similarly, when asked about a 2012 interview on *TMZ*, in which he joked about the tape, Bollea explained that what *TMZ* was trying to do was to provide character-driven entertainment, comparable to when he used to perform in the wrestling ring (Gardner, 2016). Bollea contended that his past media comments and appearances were acceptable to him and did not constitute invasions of his privacy because they were appearances he made *in character*, as Hulk Hogan.

In an exercise of self-definition, Bollea further detailed the distinction between Terry, the man, and Hogan, the character. Under questioning from his own attorney, Bollea explained:

> Well, Terry Bollea is a normal person, um, wrestling is his job, is what Hulk, Terry Bollea does for a living.
> Um, I don't argue. I'm not loud. I'm pretty soft spoken to a fault. Um, don't know how to really say "no," even though I'm learning how to say "no" to my kids. Sometimes I've been at fault with saying "yes" when I probably shoulda said "no."
> But it's the character Hulk Hogan is completely opposite of Terry Bollea. Um, the only similarities to me are, maybe sometimes the look, and you know for different reasons I wear a bandana on my head as Hulk Hogan cause that's his established look and sometimes I, sometimes I wear a bandana as Terry Bollea for other reasons.

Bollea, therefore, defined himself not only as a person separate from the persona of Hogan but also as someone who is characteristically opposite, contrasting, and dissimilar to his public character. Hulk is not, he claims, Terry, and, further, Terry and Hulk are nothing alike.

Even their physical self-presentation differs, according to Bollea. Whereas Hulk is known for donning his bandana as a stylistic trademark, Bollea claimed that he sometimes wears a bandana in his day-to-day life (he was wearing one when testifying to this point) not for style but because he lacks "self-confidence" about his "exceptionally large head" and baldness. "Hulk Hogan is different," Bollea explained, "because I'm Hulk Hogan and I wear the bandana and it's part of the wardrobe when I first introduce him. I get to the ring, and I rip the bandana off and I'm in character as Hulk Hogan." In his personal life, Bollea stated, "it's totally different . . . it's like a confidence thing or it's a personal thing."

The line of questioning centered on Bollea's appearance and physicality came to a surprising crescendo during one memorable exchange in which *Gawker* attorney, Michael Sullivan, questioned Bollea about why the publication of a video depicting him in sexual activity would cause him emotional distress, since he had previously openly engaged in sexual discussions on former-friend Bubba the Love Sponge's radio show:

Sullivan: Do you have any doubt as you sit in that witness stand today that you were discussing the length of your penis on Bubba's radio program? Any doubt?

Bollea: Well, it's not mine, because mine isn't that size, but we were discussing the length of Hulk Hogan's.

Sullivan: Seriously? So

Bollea: No, seriously, I do not have a 10-inch penis. No, I do not. Seriously.

Sullivan:	Ok, fair enough. So what you're telling us is you were discussing
Bollea:	Believe that. Seriously.
Sullivan:	Hulk Hogan's penis? Right?
Bollea:	Excuse me?
Sullivan:	You were discussing Hulk Hogan's penis.
Bollea:	Yeah, because Terry Bollea's penis is not 10 inches, like you're trying to say.

Bollea cleaves not only his public and private thoughts, motivations, and experiences from those of Hogan but also his own physical, bodily self. Bollea described the character of Hogan as having a physique that differs significantly from his own. In doing so, Bollea delineates a deep and fully severed split between public self-display and private (bodily) truth, which, in its directness, acknowledges the falsity of the public performance. Namely, Bollea's testimony reveals that his past comments made in character, as Hulk Hogan, were not accurate representations of himself, Terry Bollea, although they may have been intended to be interpreted as such.

Bollea's testimony further emphasized the distinction between self and persona when the wrestler stated that he considered it "part of the deal" as a celebrity that his "character," Hulk Hogan, had lost his anonymity. Sullivan pressed Bollea about this point on cross-examination, asking, "Are you concerned about Hulk Hogan's privacy?" to which Bollea replied:

I'm concerned, but it's pretty much take the good with the bad. You realize that when you're a character, um, they're gonna invade what if there was privacy, you know, if Hulk Hogan had any privacy, you kind of give that up when you walk out the front door as a character.

You know, I'd love to have privacy in my car, on a cell phone or something, as Hulk Hogan but you know, people take pictures and stuff like that. I walk out in public and, I went to a Rays game and went to the bathroom and everybody's calling me, "Hulk Hogan, Hulk Hogan" and I turn around, I'm standing at the urinal and somebody's taking a picture of me.

So I'm concerned about Hulk Hogan's privacy but you kind of give it away. So it is a concern, but it really doesn't matter anyway cause once you walk out the front door as Hulk Hogan, you know, your anonymity is given up and there's really no privacy anymore when you work in the public.

. . .

This is the cost of doing business, like I was trying to explain to you. You give it up but in the privacy of your own home, I'm not Hulk Hogan, so I don't have to worry about that. In the privacy of my own home I'm Terry Bollea. And nobody invades my privacy of my own home where I'm in a private setting, where I'm with my friends. . . . When I leave my house, everybody thinks I'm Hulk Hogan.

Bollea's statement attempted to establish a distinction between his own desired anonymity, as Terry, and his acceptance of the lack of anonymity as a public persona, Hulk. Here, Bollea asserted that he was *almost always* acting as Hulk Hogan, with one important caveat. He considered himself the Hulk in all circumstances except when in the privacy of his own home. This testimony establishes a critical point, one that Bollea's attorneys would argue throughout the trial, namely the idea that Bollea was *himself* within the domestic space of the home and, therefore, that the home was a place in which Bollea could enjoy a reasonable expectation of privacy.

Bollea's team claimed that he essentially *became* Hogan the moment he walked out his front door. Bollea's attorney worked to clarify this point, asking him to describe the circumstances in which he is "himself" and not Hulk Hogan. Bollea explained:

> Over the years, it was pretty much a wrestling related character, but as the years have passed by, I've realized that the moment I leave my home to go get the mail, nobody says, "Hey Terry, how you doing?" Everybody goes, "Hey Hulk, how you doing?" or "Hey Hogan," so when I'm away from my house, it's pretty much 24- hours a day when I'm not at home because no one calls me Terry anywhere. It's always, "Hey Hulk, how you doing? We love you," or "You shoulda lost," or, "You're the greatest wrestler." So it's always Hulk Hogan when people see me out, away from my home.
>
> . . .
>
> I mean, there are a few places, a few relatives, um, when I go to where my children live and I'm in their house I can definitely be Terry Bollea. Um, but other than that it's nowadays pretty limited, you know, cause the Hulk Hogan character is known worldwide so it's hard not to be Hulk Hogan. Everybody calls me Hulk Hogan everywhere I go.

This testimony positioned Bollea as a private person within the private space of his residence. In doing so, it bolstered Bollea's legal claims, given that the video tape of him engaged in sexual relations took place within the domestic sphere of the home. Yet this testimony also claims that Terry Bollea is almost never himself. He is, instead, in virtually every situation, in character. He lives the majority of his life, even when he is not intentionally performing, *as* Hulk Hogan. What, then, do we make of this character's public words and actions? How can we assess their validity and meaning?

The notion that Bollea was almost always Hogan raised questions about statements made publicly, in character, that did not align with statements Bollea made under oath during a pre-trial deposition. When confronted with these contradictions, Bollea maintained that he never lied, but rather "embellished," took "artistic liberty," or made statements "in character" (Gardner, 2016). *Gawker*'s attorney pressed him about these claims under cross-examination.

The following exchanges revolve around the issue of whether Bollea watched the sex tape when he learned of its existence, a point he later denied:

Sullivan: Now, there you tell the viewers of *VH1 Big Morning Buzz* not that you saw a minute [of the tape], but that you saw the full minute and 40-some seconds of the tape. Right?

Bollea: Yes sir.

Sullivan: Were you being truthful with the viewers of that program on that day?

Bollea: Well, that statement's not truthful. That's the same day as the media tour. That's the same day that the news was broken to me on the phone from *TMZ* and, as Hulk Hogan, to the best of, I can look at this and say I was probably in the Hulk Hogan mode, try to get through the day, try to figure out what's going on, I'm not gonna say cover my ass mode cause there was nothing to cover, but I just was in the Hulk Hogan mode, trying to get through the day and trying to get through the interview and that was not a truthful statement, as Hulk Hogan, on camera.

Sullivan: I see. So when you are in Hulk Hogan mode, rules, things like telling the truth, do not apply? Is that how it works?

Bollea: Well, as Hulk Hogan I've said I slammed an elephant and served on a tiger shark and, you know, body slammed Moby Dick so, and I also said I pulled a bumper off a Cadillac jack, so it gives you artistic liberty when you're Hulk Hogan to be a character. It's entertainment.

Bollea's testimony reveals a troubling point about the consequences of discursive self-cleaving. Whether or not Bollea believes he is lying when making these contradictory statements, acceptance of Bollea's rationale opens a problematic loophole. Here, we see how self-cleaving rhetoric offers the publicly performed self as a scapegoat for potentially damaging or even legally problematic claims. Now this persona play may be an effective rhetorical strategy when dealing with the press, promoting a product, or engaging with fans on social media, but what happens when these conflicting claims are held up to scrutiny in court, a venue where truth and facts are of the essence? Bollea stated that he himself – not his character – was the person testifying under oath and that he, Terry Bollea, didn't lie. The jury, it seems, believed him. Bollea ultimately prevailed in his lawsuit and was awarded a six-figure settlement. The outcome of the case proved that a civil jury could be swayed by self-cleaving as a legal line of reasoning. It was an outcome that many reporters and media organizations found shocking, and one whose full implications were only beginning to emerge (Knappenberger, 2017).

Reality, Fame, and Power

The significant financial award and accompanying ruling in the Bollea v. *Gawker* case seemed to affirm that Bollea was a wronged victim and *Gawker* an exploitative media organization. Yet, for some observers, the ruling did little to settle a creeping sense of dread (Knappenberger, 2017). Journalists and free-speech advocates worried that the case was an ill omen for an unrestrained and fulsome press and a gateway to unchecked power for any public person who might be willing to engage in similar denials. "Unexpectedly," wrote Ravi Somaiya for *The New York Times*, with the *Bollea v. Gawker* case, "we veer into a legal, moral, and philosophical question that involves the very nature of who we are, or at least who Mr. Bollea actually is" (Somaiya, 2016). Because if a public person can simply claim that words said in the past, even in the legal context of a deposition or trial, were said "in character" as a plausible excuse for their lack of veracity, then the entire foundation of the legal enterprise – and the journalistic one – is rocked from its mantle.

Hulk Hogan rose to fame in the wrestling ring, where taunts, exaggerations, half-truths, and blatant falsehoods are all acceptable and where it is the reaction of the audience, Shannon Bow O'Brien writes in her book on kayfabe and public life, that functions "as the barometer for the truth rather than objective standards that gauge accuracy" (2020, p. 3). Hogan's existence, as a character, was rooted in kayfabe, grounded in the manipulation of truth and fact, and birthed in a world where apologies and admissions are character flaws that break the illusion and spoil the fun, a world where "the more forcefully you argue a position, the more truthful it is" (O'Brien, 2020, p. 9). But while the discursive realm of popular culture may welcome and profit from contrivances and embellished fictions, the legal system, at least in theory, demands a distinction between fact and fantasy.

So it was in the 1990s, when Terry Bollea faced accusations of steroid use, that he testified to at trial (Barrasso, 2021). At that time, the ensuring revelations threatened the Hogan brand with their acknowledgment that Hogan's cartoonishly muscular physique was not a result of his being heroically strong but of his very human choice to use illegal performance enhancers (Chard & Litherland, 2019). Confronted with the rigors of testimony, Bollea's kayfabe was broken. In that instance, revelations of truth brought to light the actions of the man, which threatened the illusion of the character. The *Gawker* case also took place in a legal venue which required commitment to a truth that is singular, not split between worlds. But in 2016, the court sided with Bollea. Something was different this time. Even held up to the light of legal process, kayfabe reigned. Bollea was able to successfully occupy a dual position as litigant and character, as though the latter was merely a fantasy whose words and deeds were completely distinct from his own.

Bollea's success at trial prompted Nick Denton, then-editor-in-chief of *Gawker*, to ask whether it is possible, given this outcome, to ever "catch a public person out in a lie" in contemporary culture (Knappenberger, 2017). If even the courtroom is a space where discursive self-cleaving proves an effective strategy for image maintenance and consequence avoidance, how can we ever hold public figures to account? Sure, the Bollea v. *Gawker* case may seem, at first glance, like a wacky one-off, a tawdry celebrity sex tape trial. But it's not much of a reach to imagine a related, and far more sinister, scenario in which this type of rhetorical strategy could be used by someone sitting behind the defendant's table. We could imagine a celebrity accused of reckless driving, or drug possession, or tax evasion, making the case that it was their persona, not themself, who committed the crime, and therefore they should be found not guilty. Pushed to the hypothetical limit, one wonders whether a star could commit a felony and then use their persona as a legal shield. Who, then, would the jury believe? With whom would the American public side?

It turns out that this question was far less hypothetical than one would hope. In January 2016, less than two months before the jury would hear Bollea's argument, Donald Trump was campaigning to be the Republican presidential nominee, and he was asking precisely this question, out loud, very much in the open. Speaking to reporters in the lead-up to the Iowa caucus, he noted that his followers were so loyal to him that they would not waver in their support even if he committed a capital offense, stating, "I could stand in the middle of Fifth Avenue and shoot somebody, and I wouldn't lose any voters, OK? It's, like, incredible." *NPR*'s Don Gonyea reported that the reaction to Trump's statement was familiar: it riled his foes but energized his base: "His audiences love it His opponents try to use it against him – but so far, to no avail" (Dwyer, 2016).

On March 13, 2016, just three days before the jury would find in favor of Terry Bollea, Trump's spokesperson appeared on Fox News and engaged the self-cleaving rhetoric on behalf of her client, contending that sexist comments he had previously made were merely part of his act (Roy, 2016). Over the next year, the American public would be confronted, on a national level with the rhetorical strategy that Bollea had successfully tested in a Florida courtroom. Only this time, it was a politician, using his celebrity persona, first, to secure the presidency despite dozens of allegations of misogyny and sexual assault against him and, next, to govern in a way that reveled in speculation, obfuscated with so-called fake news, and purposefully untethered itself from fact. In retrospect, we can look back on *Bollea v. Gawker* as a pivotal legal moment, one which embodied and expressed a shift in public expectations around truth telling and augured a growing trend in the use of self-cleaving as a rhetorical tool of powerful men seeking to evade scrutiny.

Note

1 During the trial, video cameras were permitted in the courtroom and footage of the *Bollea v. Gawker* proceedings was made public via news and social media reports. I personally transcribed all court proceedings quoted in this chapter using video of testimony made available by Law and Crime

Network (@LawAndCrime on YouTube.com), with select quotations corroborated by reports published by ABC News, *The Atlantic*, *The Hollywood Reporter*, *The New York Times*, and NPR.

References

ABC News. (2016, March 9). Hulk Hogan grilled on the stand. *Good Morning America.*

Ahmad, T., & Swain, S. R. (2011). Celebrity rights: Protection under IP laws. *Journal of Intellectual Property Rights, 16*, 7–16.

Ang, I. (1989). *Watching Dallas*. Routledge.

Antoniou, A. K., & Akrivos, D. (2016). Hulk Hogan and the demise of *Gawker* media: Wrestling with problems of celebrity voyeurism, newsworthiness and tabloidisation. *Journal of Media Law, 8*(2), 153–172.

Barrasso, J. (2021, July 26). WWE scripted series will portray Vince McMahon's 1994 steroids trial. *Sports Illustrated*. Retrieved October 24, 2023, from https://www.si.com/wrestling/2021/07/26/wwe-scripted-series-vince-mcmahon-1994-steroids-trial

Barthes, R. (1972). *Mythologies*. Hill & Wang.

Beekman, S. (2006). *Ringside: A history of professional wrestling*. Praeger.

Ben-Zeev, A., Scharnetzki, L., Chan, L. K., & Dennehy, T. C. (2012). Hypermasculinity in the media: When men "walk into the fog" to avoid affective communication. *Psychology of Popular Media Culture, 1*(1), 53–61.

CBS/AP. (2016, March 7). Hulk Hogan: I was "completely humiliated" when *Gawker* published sex video. *CBS News*. Retrieved January 27, 2024, from https://www.cbsnews.com/news/hulk-hogan-to-take-witness-stand-in-lawsuit-against-gawker/

Chard, H., & Litherland, B. (2019). "Hollywood" Hulk Hogan. *Journal of Cinema and Media Studies, 58*(4), 21–44.

Darnell, S. C., & Wilson, B. (2006). Macho media: Unapologetic hypermasculinity in Vancouver's "talk radio for guys". *Journal of Broadcasting and Electronic Media, 50*(3), 444–466.

deCordova, R. (1990). *Picture personalities: The emergence of the star system in America*. University of Illinois Press.

Douglas, S. J., & McDonnell, A. (2019). *Celebrity: A history of fame*. New York University Press.

Drake, P. (2007). Who owns celebrity? Privacy, publicity and the legal regulation of celebrity images. In S. Redmond & S. Holmes (Eds.), *Stardom and celebrity: A reader* (pp. 219–229). Sage.

Drake, P. (2018). Celebrity, reputational capital and the media industries. In A. Elliott (Ed.), *Routledge handbook of celebrity studies*, pp. 271–284. Routledge.

Dwyer, C. (2016, January 23). Donald Trump: "I could . . . shoot somebody, and I wouldn't lose any voters". *NPR*. Retrieved October 21, 2023, from https://www.npr.org/sections/thetwo-way/2016/01/23/464129029/donald-trump-i-could-shoot-somebody-and-i-wouldnt-lose-any-voters

Dyer, R. (1986). *Heavenly bodies: Film stars and society.* Macmillan.

Dyer, R. (1991). A star is born and the construction of authenticity. In C. Gledhill (Ed.), *Stardom: Industry of desire* (pp. 132–140). Routledge.

Franklin, M. A., Anderson, D. A., & Cate, F. H. (2001). *Mass media law: Cases and materials* (6th ed.). Foundation Press.

Gamson, J. (1994). *Claims to fame: Celebrity in contemporary America.* University of California Press.

Gardner, E. (2016, March 8). Hulk Hogan grilled about sex-filled TMZ, Howard Stern interviews at *Gawker* trial. *The Hollywood Reporter.*

Higgins, M. (2019). The Donald: Media, celebrity, authenticity, and accountability. In C. Happer, A. Hoskins, & W. Merrin (Eds.), *Trump's media war* (pp. 129–141). Palgrave.

Horton, D., & Wohl, R. R. (1956). Mass communication and para-social interaction. *Psychiatry, 19,* 215–229.

Jenkins, H. (2005). "Never trust a snake": WWF wrestling as masculine melodrama. In N. Sammond (Ed.), *Steel chair to the head: The pleasure and pain of professional wrestling* (pp. 33–66). Duke University Press.

Knappenberger, B. (2017). *Nobody speak: Trials of the free press.* Netflix.

Lai, A. (2006). Glitter and grain: Aura and authenticity in the celebrity photographs of Juergen Teller. In S. Redmond & S. Holmes (Eds.), *Framing celebrity: New directions in celebrity culture* (pp. 215–230). Routledge.

Laine, E. (2018). Professional wrestling scholarship: Legitimacy and kayfabe. *The Popular Culture Studies Journal, 6*(1), 82–99.

Madigan, N. (2016, March 8). Hulk Hogan exudes calm in second day of sex tape trial against Gawker. *The New York Times.*

Madigan, N., & Somaiya, R. (2016, March 18). Hulk Hogan awarded $115 million in privacy suit against *Gawker. The New York Times.*

Magee, W. (2017, March 14). The Cult: Hulk Hogan. *Vice.*

Marsh, J. (2016, March 16). Hogan sex-tape hottie: My husband demanded I have sex with Hulk. *The New York Post.* Retrieved January 27, 2024, from https://nypost.com/2016/03/16/hogan-sex-tape-hottie-i-had-no-idea-hubby-was-filming-us/

Marshall, D. P. (1997). *Celebrity and power: Fame in contemporary culture.* University of Minnesota Press.

Mazer, S. (2005). "Real wrestling"/ "real" life. In N. Sammond (Ed.), *Steel chair to the head: The pleasure and pain of professional wrestling* (pp. 67–87). Duke University Press.

McDonnell, A. (2021). From baby bumps to border walls: Celebrity gossip magazines and the post-truth presidency. In M. Conboy & S. Eldridge (Eds.), *Global tabloid.* Routledge.

Meyers, E. (2009). "Can you handle my truth"? Authenticity and the celebrity star image. *The Journal of Popular Culture, 42*(5), 890–907.

Mosher, D. L., & Sirkin, M. (1984). Measuring a macho personality constellation. *Journal of Research in Personality, 18*(2), 150–163.

Nordhaus, J. E. (1999). Celebrities' rights to privacy: How far should the paparazzi be allowed to go? *The Review of Litigation, 18*(2), 285–315.

O'Brien, S. B. (2020). *Donald Trump and the kayfabe presidency: Professional wrestling in the White House.* Palgrave.

Patterson, J. (2016, March 16). Scandalous details revealed about radio personality's sex life during Hogan trial. *News Channel 8, WFLA Tampa Bay.* Retrieved January 27, 2024, from https://www.wfla.com/news/scandalous-details-revealed-about-radio-personalitys-sex-life-during-hogan-trial/

Roy, J. (2016, March 15). Trump spokesperson says it was his TV character, not him, who made all those sexist comments. *The Cut.* Retrieved October 24, 2023, from https://www.thecut.com/2016/03/trump-blames-his-tv-character-for-sexist-remarks.html

Schickel, R. (1986). *Intimate strangers: The culture of celebrity.* Fromm International Publishing Co.

Somaiya, R. (2016, March 8). When is Hulk Hogan not Hulk Hogan? *The New York Times.*

Thompson, D. (2018, February 23). The most expensive comment in internet history? *The Atlantic.*

Winer, A. (2016, March 17). Web ad to be used against Hulk Hogan in trial. *WFTS Tampa Bay.*

2 Mr. Trump // Donald J. Trump

While Terry Bollea was ensnared in a legal battle with *Gawker*, Donald Trump was campaigning to become president of the United States. For many Americans, Trump's decision to vie for the Republican Party's 2015 nomination was unexpected, even a bit surprising. Here was a man who was known best for his real-estate deals, flashy persona, and popular reality series, *The Apprentice* (NBC), where he performed as the mogul-host and coined the catchphrase "You're fired" during the weekly elimination of hopeful contestants. Trump was a figure of the popular culture, the tabloid world, not the political one. Most voters would strain to recall how, in the 1980s, Trump paid upwards of $80,000 to place full-page advertisements in New York newspapers attacking five Black and Latino teens, falsely accused of assaulting a jogger in Central Park; the ad dubbed the boys "wild criminals" and called for the return of the death penalty (Waxman, 2019). Few would remember that Trump had attempted a presidential run in 2000 (Trump, 2000) or that he appeared as a featured speaker at the Conservative Political Action Conference (CPAC) in the lead-up to the 2012 election. But they *did* know him from television, the papers, and, yes, even from the world of professional wrestling.

This chapter considers the emergence of Donald Trump's self-cleaving rhetoric in the years leading up to his presidential bid and goes on to examine his image management strategies during his 2016 campaign for president. I also consider Trump's response to one specific event that threatened to derail his political career: the release of a video depicting him making lewd comments about women while on the set of *Access Hollywood*. Trump's public comments following the release of the *Access Hollywood* tape demonstrate a nuanced version of self-cleaving, in which Trump attempts to save face through multiple, subtle, and interwoven discourses related to "locker room talk." Here, we can see a practice of self-cleaving that relies not on the eschewing of one's celebrity character in favor of a "true" self but on a pattern of language use intended to render deniable the speaker's prior comments through the activation of multiple, situationally contextualized presentations of self. Considered alongside Trump and his team's rhetoric of "fake news" and "alternative facts," we see

DOI: 10.4324/9781003380139-3

how discursive self-cleaving contributes to a post-truth politic, one which tests the limits of journalists' reporting and citizen competence.

Mr. Trump Runs for President

Long before he was elected president of the United States, Donald Trump was a figure of exaggeration and innuendo, a man whose personal mythmaking was built on sprinklings of half-truths with a dash of glitter thrown in for good measure. Stories about Trump – his childhood, his wealth, his marriages and divorces – were repeated again and again, passed along like a decades-long game of telephone by an eager media. Courting the attention of the tabloid press throughout the 1980s and 1990s, Trump was known for developing New York real estate, his flashy public persona, and his knack for generating tabloid stories about, well, himself.

Details of Donald Trump's "lifelong habit of attempting to create and sell his own version of reality" were widely reported: he had claimed Trump Tower was several stories taller than it actually was, exaggerated his financial position, overstated his ownership role in Trump International Hotel & Tower Waikiki Beach Walk, stretched the truth about how quickly units in his Las Vegas hotel sold out, overvalued properties based on his own opinion, denied debts he owed, and generally took an extremely optimistic view when valuing his assets (Haberman & Martin, 2017; Peterson-Withorn, 2016). He also admitted to using what he called "truthful hyperbole" when outlining details of his personal history in his book *The Art of the Deal* (Haberman & Martin, 2017).

Trump's theatricality and penchant for exaggeration cast him as an ideal character for the world of professional wrestling. In the 1980s, as Trump offered up his casinos as venues for the fights, he also began to appear *in* the ring (Dawsey, 2017). Trump participated in the body slams and the trash talking while cultivating his persona, Mr. Trump, who just so happened to be a wealthy businessman (O'Brien, 2020). Hundred-dollar bills dropped onto the audience when Trump won a match. When he was inducted into the WWE Hall of Fame in 2013, "money, money" was played on speakers and dollar bills were displayed on large screens (Dawsey, 2017). Like Bollea's Hulk, the Mr. Trump persona came to dominate the public image of Donald Trump, the man. But while Bollea's character has, to date, functioned almost exclusively in the realm of popular culture, Donald Trump and his Mr. Trump persona have, over the past decade, become dominant figures in the American political landscape.

By the early 2000s, Trump was enjoying a renewed wave of fame as the host of the popular NBC reality competition show *The Apprentice*. As in the wrestling ring, the show portrayed Mr. Trump as a character, an uber-successful mogul, a paragon of influence, and a business acumen who was outrageously wealthy and totally in control (Poniewozik, 2019). He was depicted flying around the Manhattan skyline on helicopters brandishing the Trump logo, introducing young businesspeople to his seemingly vast network of renowned associates and acting as a decisive boss man. Never mind that news reports suggested that his businesses had been mismanaged, losing more than a billion dollars over a ten-year period or that he himself had only narrowly avoided bankruptcy (Cassidy, 2019). As Patrick Radden Keefe writes in *The New Yorker*, the show beamed the Mr. Trump archetype into millions of viewers' living rooms on a weekly basis. And although reality TV is not actually real, it presents itself as such. The show's producer, Mark Burnett, notes, reality TV is more akin to "dramality," a blend of showmanship and reality, created through editing and the careful use of music, camera angles, and narrative to convey emotion and create drama (Radden Keefe, 2018). By featuring and bolstering the Mr. Trump character, *The Apprentice* played a key role in revitalizing Trump's image in the public's mind during the years preceding his presidential campaign (Radden Keefe, 2018).

As Trump turned his eye away from network television and towards politics, he continued to demonstrate a willingness to traffic in speculation, innuendo, and falsehoods. Indeed, it was his persistent espousal of the racist conspiracy theory known as birtherism, which claimed Barack Obama, the first African American president of the United States, was not born in the country, that catapulted Trump into the national political news in 2011 (ABC, 2016). The theory of birtherism contends not only that Obama was born abroad, and therefore ineligible to be president, but also that he was secretly a Muslim, planning to corrupt the country from within its most vaulted chamber of power (Sewer, 2020). Although Donald Trump was not the first to promote birtherism, he popularized it, embracing the speculation and pushing himself into the spotlight in the process, through interviews with Fox News (Sewer, 2020). As political pressure grew, President Obama publicly released his birth certificate in an effort to stem the speculation. Nevertheless, Trump's promulgation of the birther conspiracy served as a stepping stone, one from which he propelled himself into the political arena and, in doing so, rallied anti-Obama Republicans to his side. Though birtherism was ultimately exposed as a lie, Trump successfully used the publicity generated by the scandal to position himself as a truth teller, a renegade who would speak up and reveal that which those in power would prefer to remain hidden.

Specifically, Trump fashioned himself as the antidote to political correctness – a term he used to denote a polished, knowing political facade. Using vernacular folksiness, repetition, foul language, and expressive gestures, Trump eschewed the conventions of political speech, presenting himself as someone who did not hold back, whose expressions were a true representation of his inner self (Montgomery et al., 2019). Trump embraced his political offensiveness as a tacit claim on sincerity, allowing him to embody a quality of truthiness, without having to actually speak the truth (Montgomery, 2017). Sincerity is not the same thing as authenticity, but they are linked. *Sincerity* is about a cohesion between the inner self and outward expression, self-display without concealment (Scannell, 1996, p. 56). Sincerity may also involve the verbalization of that which might normally remain unsaid, the revelation of which contributes to the rapport between speaker and listener. Trump fostered a populist discourse rooted in a performance of sincerity, rather than based on fact, and it was precisely this appeal that proved crucially effective in cultivating and energizing his base (Montgomery, 2017).

In 2015, Donald Trump announced his bid for the American presidency. Throughout the ensuing campaign, Trump continued to cultivate his image as an unfiltered outsider, who defied political conventions and told it like he saw it. One of the key sites where he enacted this "realness" was the social media platform Twitter (now X), where he posted from his @realDonaldTrump handle. Trump used Twitter to rhetorically construct his own version of reality. For instance, his handle itself uses the word *real* to imply the existence of false accounts, imposters, fakers, or those who might otherwise try to lie about or imitate Trump himself. It also suggests that other politicians are not being "real" with voters, in their public personas and statements, a point Trump reiterated throughout his campaign, dubbing his opponents "Lying Ted [Cruz]" and "Crooked Hillary [Clinton]." Finally, the handle advances the notion that Trump is speaking to the public as his "real" self, an unfiltered, honest, forthright account. The handle tells us he will not hold back – he will speak directly to his followers. The @realDonaldTrump handle, therefore, provides Trump with a discursive space in which he can perform being authentic, sincere, and forthright (McDonnell & Wheeler, 2019). In doing so, Trump once again stakes his claim on truthfulness and suggests that anyone who may question him is not to be believed. On the campaign trail, Trump reinforced this messaging of "realness," highlighting his reputation as a successful businessman in contrast to his rival politicians, jostling for support in a crowded Republican field. And this message resonated with voters; a 2016 Gallup poll found that his Republican supporters cited his outsider status and business experience as top reasons for their favoring Trump (Newport & Saad, 2016). Trump also honed his claims on "realness" to deflect criticism against him, which was growing alongside his chances of becoming the GOP nominee.

One element of Trump's record that came under scrutiny was his treatment of, and comments about, women and girls. By spring 2015, more than 50 women had come forward to accuse Trump of making sexual or degrading comments about their faces and bodies, engaging in inappropriate workplace conduct, and issuing unwelcome sexual and physical advances (Barbaro & Twohey, 2016). Former contestants in the Miss Universe Pageant, a Trump-owned entity, reported that he had unexpectedly kissed them on the lips. An associate recalled a time when he had sought feedback about his 16-year-old daughter Ivanka's appearance, asking, "Don't you think my daughter's hot? She's hot, right?" (Barbaro & Twohey, 2016). At the same time, contestants on *The Apprentice* reported that Trump had regularly made crude comments about the bodies of female contestants and female staffers. One *Apprentice* employee reported hearing Trump say, "How about those boobs? Wouldn't you like to f*ck her?" (Radden Keefe, 2018).

Trump pushed back, claiming that the comments he had made about women were part of his act, made "in character," simply an element of his role as a reality television star and entertainer (Graham, 2016). On one occasion, when asked by a reporter whether he could understand the concern from parents of young girls, Trump responded, "A lot of that was done for the purpose of entertainment, there's nobody that has more respect for women than I do." In March 2016, campaign spokesperson Katrina Pearson appeared as a guest on Fox News and defended allegations that Trump had made lewd sexual comments and remarks about women's appearance, stating, "I really don't think [these comments are] going to be a problem. A lot of those statements [are] what Mr. Trump made as a television character. So I don't think that some of that is going to stick" (Roy, 2016).

During this period, we see Trump engage in the type of discursive self-cleaving detailed in the previous chapter, directly marking his Mr. Trump persona as a television character in ways that allow him to disentangle his "real" self from his past comments. Trump brands his previous statements as theatrics, fodder for the reality TV crowd. In doing so, he acknowledges his audiences' media savvy, their awareness that reality TV is not, in fact, real. Everyone knows, as James Poniewozik would later write in the *New York Times*, that "being real," in the context of television, "is not the same thing as being honest. To be real is to be the most entertaining, provocative form of yourself. It is to say what you want, without caring whether your words are kind or responsible – or true – but only whether you want to say them" (2019). Only a rube, Trump's denials suggested, would believe that reality TV stars mean what they say. It's all an over-the-top show, designed to draw ratings.

When asked by one reporter whether he would try to "tone down" his rhetoric as a presidential candidate, Trump replied, "It's not a question of trying, it's very easy." Easy because, Trump suggests, his natural inclination, his "real" personality, is far more demure, respectful, and staid than that of his TV persona (Snyder & Clerkin, 2016). In this way, candidate Trump managed to have his cake and eat it too, benefiting from the glamor and outsider appeal of his Mr. Trump image while using that persona as a shield against criticism of his past statements. But in October 2016, one news story broke that was so compelling, it threatened to break through Trump's carefully honed defenses.

The Access Hollywood Tape

On October 7, 2016, just weeks before the presidential election, a September 2005 video featuring Trump, on a bus inside the NBC lot, speaking with *Access Hollywood* co-anchor Billy Bush, was released by reporter David Fahrenthold in a story for *The Washington Post*.[1] The video depicts Trump, on a hot microphone, making misogynistic remarks about women and expressing a desire to kiss and grab them by the genitalia without their consent. Trump's words on the tape would become infamous, repeated ad nauseum on cable news and across social and mainstream news media.

Trump's comments on the video immediately triggered a political and media firestorm. *Politico* would later describe the ensuing fallout as "apocalyptic" (Alberta, 2019). GOP Senate majority leader Mitch McConnell called Trump's remarks "repugnant" and "unacceptable" (Fahrenthold, 2016). Arizona senator and former Republican presidential candidate John McCain withdrew his support, joining a growing group of more than two dozen senators publicly announcing that they would not vote for Trump (Alberta, 2019; Phelps et al., 2016). Pundits speculated as to how this "October surprise" would affect Trump's upcoming debate against Democratic nominee Hillary Clinton, scheduled to take place just two days later, and his viability in the general election.

The revelation of the *Access Hollywood* tape can be understood as what sociologist Erving Goffman calls an *inopportune intrusion*, a moment when the audience inadvertently enters the backstage (Goffman, 1959, p. 209). Goffman describes the sociable arrangement of everyday interaction and the ways in which we present ourselves to manage those interactions; according to Goffman, social interaction takes place in various regions. Back regions, or backstage areas, are often blocked off to or separate from public spaces; they are regions whose entry is limited to those who possess a special kind of membership. On the "front stage" we perform our selves in a "general and fixed fashion . . . designed to incorporate and exemplify the officially accredited values of the society" (Goffman, 1959, pp. 22, 35). But "backstage," the performance may temporarily drop; backstage behavior may be more casual, and it may include "profanity, open sexual remarks . . . playful aggressivity and 'kidding'" (Goffman, 1959, p. 128). In the *Access Hollywood* tape, Trump is quite literally backstage, on a studio lot, but he is also operating in a *backstage region*, a place away from public view, "where the performer can reliably expect that no member of the audience will intrude" (Goffman, 1959, pp. 112–113). Trump and Bush converse in a comfortable style, characteristic of a backstage environment; their language is casual, colloquial, and friendly, containing crosstalk between the two men, along with profanity, and humor.

During the first part of the conversation, Trump discusses his attempts to initiate a sexual relationship with Nancy O'Dell, Bush's then co-host of *Access Hollywood*. What follows is a partial transcript of the tape's dialogue (*The Washington Post*, 2016).

Unknown: She used to be great; she's still very beautiful.
Trump: I moved on her actually. You know she was down on Palm Beach. I moved on her, and I failed. I'll admit it. I did try and f*ck her, she was married.

Unknown: Woah. That's huge news there.
Trump: No, no, Nancy. No this was [inaudible] and I moved on her very heavily in fact I took her out furniture shopping. She wanted to get some furniture. I said I'll show you where they have some nice furniture. I took her out – I moved on her like a bitch. I couldn't get there and she was married. Then all-of-a-sudden I see her, she's now got the big phony tits and everything. She's totally changed her look.

As the conversation continues, Bush and Trump are heard discussing other women. Here, Trump and Bush notice Adrienne Zucker, the actress who will later escort them to the set (Fahrenthold, 2016). Trump describes non-consensual, sexual acts, including grabbing women by their genitalia, and expresses a sense of entitlement in being able to make such advances due to his status as a reality television star and famous figure.

Bush: Sheesh, your girl's hot as shit. In the purple.
Multiple voices: Whoah. Yes. Whoah.
Bush: Yes. The Donald has scored. Woah my man.
Trump: Look at you. You are a pussy.
Bush: You gotta get the thumbs up.
Trump: Maybe it's a different one.
Bush: It better not be the publicist. No, it's, it's her.
Trump: Yeah that's her with the gold. I better use some Tic Tacs just in case I start kissing her. You know I'm automatically attracted to beautiful. I just start kissing them. It's like a magnet. Just kiss. I don't even wait. And when you're a star they let you do it. You can do anything.
Bush: Whatever you want.
Trump: Grab them by the pussy. You can do anything.
Bush: Yeah those legs. All I can see is the legs.

Later in the footage, an important shift occurs. Trump and Bush begin to exit the bus and are therefore no longer operating in a purely backstage area. As they exit the private region of the bus, they enter the semi-public realm of the studio set, in which other individuals may enter. "Perhaps just as telling as what's said on the video is how Trump's manner shifts from when he's talking behind the bus door to when the door opens and he steps out to greet Zucker," writes Jeffrey Fleishman for the *LA Times*. "His voice lifts an octave and its inflections are softer, as if, in his parlance, he has moved from the locker room into the light of more discerning eyes" (2016). Indeed, as actress Arianne Zucker enters the frame, the conversation continues, but takes a notable turn.

[Mr. Trump exits the bus and greets actress Arianne Zucker]

Trump:	Hello, how are you? Hi.
Zucker:	Hi Mr. Trump. How are you?
Trump:	Nice seeing you. Terrific. Terrific. You know Billy Bush?
Bush:	Hello nice to see you. How are you doing Arianne?
Zucker:	I'm doing very well thank you. [Addressing Trump] Are you ready to be a soap star?
Trump:	We're ready. Let's go. Make me a soap star.
Bush:	How about a little hug for the Donald, he just got off the bus?
Zucker:	Would you like a little hug darling?
Trump:	Absolutely. Melania said this was okay.
Bush:	How about a little hug for the Bushy, I just got off the bus? Here we go, here we go. Excellent.
Bush:	Well you've got a good co-star here.
Trump:	Good. After you. Come on Billy, don't be shy.
Bush:	Soon as a beautiful woman shows up he just, he takes off. This always happens.

As Goffman notes, moments of transition between regions are critical to observe impression management in that they make visible the shifting modes of presentation (1959, p. 121). As Trump and Bush exit the backstage, their tone shifts. The vulgarity, profanity, and machismo of the private conversation are replaced with a flirty, overly familiar friendliness, as the pair attempt to charm Zucker. The two also support one another's self-presentation in the exchange, with Trump asking Zucker if she knows Bush, Bush requesting Zucker hug Trump, and then Bush explaining Trump's reaction to the sight of a "beautiful woman" to Zucker. The dynamic between the two men is a mutually supportive one, and their cooperation in this exchange works to suggest the validity of their statements.

But the move from back to front stage does not only operate within the studio set, from the backstage of the bus to the front stage (or semi-private) region of the studio lot. Indeed, if the talk were limited to those regions, as it had been from the tape was filmed in 2005 until the time it was released in 2016, it would have likely remained largely inconsequential as a matter of public debate. What occurs upon the publication of the tape by members of the media is another, much larger shift. Here, we see Donald Trump's (and Billy Bush's) words transition from the backstage into a very public, front stage region – that of the political and media public sphere.

Once Trump's backstage talk was revealed to the public, the American people were confronted with a new image of the "real" Republican nominee. The self-cleaving rhetoric engaged by Trump in the statements detailed at the start of this chapter functioned by highlighting the public self as a means of generating plausible deniability of statements made in public, thus contending that one's private and true thoughts differ from those made openly. But the release of the *Access Hollywood* video posed a new and distinct challenge for Trump, as it depicted him speaking and acting in a scenario where he seemed to be his open and unmitigated self. Because the video presented an interaction in which Trump appeared unguarded, unmediated, and therefore apparently authentic, it blocked his ability to deny his statements by claiming that he was acting in character.[2] Trump and his team now faced the task of renewing the image of him that voters would hold in their minds come election day. Trump needed, in other words, to save face.

To *save face* is to engage in a form of image coordination that either anticipates threats and deflects them accordingly or attempts to mitigate damage from previous faux pas. *Face*, in this context, can be understood literally as one's visage, but also as a metaphor "for one's social value" (Goffman, 1967, p. 5). "A person may be said to *have*, or *be in*, or *maintain* face," Goffman writes, "when the line he effectively takes presents an image of him that is internally consistent, that is supported by judgments and evidence" (1967, p. 6). When face is lost, participants engage in a "corrective process" to save or regain it. The offender "is given a chance to correct for the offense and re-establish the expressive order" (Goffman, 1967, p. 20). In the hours and weeks following the release of the *Access Hollywood* tape, we can trace Donald Trump's attempts to save face. His actions demonstrate first, an understanding that face had been lost, and second, an awareness that he must regain face in or to maintain his standing in the presidential race and in the public sphere more broadly.

Trump's first face-saving effort was one traditionally used in politics and public relations: he issued an apology via video, in which he stated:

> I've never said I'm a perfect person, nor pretended to be someone that I'm not. I've said and done things I regret, and the words released today on this more than a decade-old video are one of them. Anyone who knows me, knows these words don't reflect who I am. I said it, I was wrong, and I apologize.

An apology is generally understood as a sincere effort to repair a breach, and, if it is perceived as such by the audience, the performer will regain face, repairing his public status. If the apology is not deemed sincere or fulsome enough, it may be questioned. Or, additionally, if the revelation of the backstage behavior rings true or seems to reflect the "real" self that has been hidden on the front stage, an apology may not be sufficient to reconcile the audience's new knowledge of the performer's unmitigated words. For some voters, this may have been the case with Trump, and criticism persisted (Rhodes et al., 2020).

Locker Room Talk

Trump's campaign quickly issued an additional statement, using a new, face-saving strategy. In it, Trump called the comments "locker room banter, a private conversation that took place many years ago." He also noted that former-president Bill Clinton had "said far worse to me on the golf course – not even close" (Fahrenthold, 2016; Johnston, 2016). Trump's placing Clinton's comments in the context of the golf course may, at first glance, appear an off-the-cuff remark, one which reinforces the two men's positions as powerful individuals who circulate in the same social circles. Yet Trump's use of this specific location to position Clinton's alleged remarks also sets the stage for what would become his primary public defense against the *Access Hollywood* video. By situating Clinton's remarks in the setting of the golf course, he marks those comments as having taken place in an arena that is sports related and, most importantly, male dominated. Since its modern development in the 18th century, golf has largely been a men's game, a gendered dynamic reinforced through the establishment of all-male clubs, such as golfing societies.

Then, on October 9, Donald Trump participated in a presidential debate alongside the Democratic presidential nominee Hillary Clinton. During the debate, when asked about his conduct by co-moderator Anderson Cooper, who noted that Trump's words on the tape described a form of sexual assault, Trump doubled down on his use of the phrase "locker room talk." "No, I didn't say that at all," said Trump. "I don't think you understood what was – this was locker room talk. I'm not proud of it. I apologize to my family. I apologize to the American people. Certainly I'm not proud of it. But this is locker room talk." When further pressed by Cooper, Trump remarked, "I have great respect for women. Nobody has more respect for women than I do" (Keneally, 2017).

In describing his language as "locker room talk," Trump explicitly marks his comments on the *Access Hollywood* tape as backstage talk. He acknowledges the region specificity of his words and uses the region itself as an explanation for his speech, a defense of its explicitness. The locker room is a gendered, sequestered space. We may think of other, similarly gendered and cloistered spaces – the lady's restroom or beauty parlor, the men's barber shop or cigar lounge. At times, similar spaces may also be defined by race or religious affiliation. In these types of spaces, participants may engage in modes of talk that adhere to the modalities and practices of that space, and which may be perceived as freer or more candid because the space itself serves as an insulated region, one which is set apart, and hidden from, the ears of outsiders. One study of African American hair salons, for instance, contends that participants in these spaces collaborate, negotiate, construct, and transmit their understanding of the world through the cultural activity of the salon, through a discourse known as "shoptalk" (Majors, 2003). In addition to the nature of the region itself, the shared identities and lived experiences of group members, perceived or actual, also contribute to the sense of freedom within the discursive realm.

Entry to a locker room is restricted by gender and membership to a team, school, or club. The locker room is physically blocked off, hidden from view of outsiders. What occurs, and what is said, in the space of the locker room is therefore protected. In his analysis of conversation in these spaces, Curry writes, "The men's locker room is enshrined in sports mythology as a bastion of privilege and a center of fraternal bonding. The stereotyped view of the locker room is that it is a retreat from the outside world" (1991, p. 119). These are enclaves that, physically and discursively, reveal men *to* one another, *away* from the outside world (Jimerson, 2001, p. 328). For these reasons, locker rooms facilitate private, even intimate, conversations within all-male groups.

Linguistically, it is far easier to characterize stereotypes around feminine speech than masculine, in large part because gender norms have long positioned masculine speech as normative, a baseline against which other speech can be measured (Spender, 1980). But in scenarios where masculinity is heightened, as in all-male speech groups, men may use language in specific ways designed to draw attention to their masculine identity, exert superiority, and resist social constraints around normative behavior. For example, gender stereotypes suggest that men are less talkative than women, but in hypermasculine discourse regions, masculinity may be performed through bombast (Ben-Zeev et al., 2012). The expression of excessive emotion through violent, sexualized, unapologetic, or otherwise aggressive speech can also be a discursive tactic for claiming masculinity (Darnell & Wilson, 2006). We see examples of this on "shock-jock" talk radio (Darnell & Wilson, 2006) and in hip-hop and heavy metal music (Grant, 1996).

The realm of sport is also one in which gender roles are performed and players, especially males, bond with one another through the display of masculinity (Curry, 1991; Vaynman et al., 2020). Within the space of the locker room, the social confines of speech are relaxed. Male speech is free to adopt transgressive markers, including profanity, innuendo, and hostility towards women and homosexual men. This discursive space promotes competition, reaffirms one's own sense of self, affords an opportunity for homosocial bonding, and enhances one's social and team status (Curry, 1991).

The reinforcement of homosocial bonds in all-male speech groups often rely on the use of degrading language, profanity, and bragging and boasting (Vaynman et al., 2020). When Trump claims that Bill Clinton has made inappropriate comments to him on a golf course, he is drawing on a commonly held understanding that sports arenas, especially all-male arenas, are spaces where such language is more openly used than in mixed-gender spaces. Indeed, scholarship suggests that locker room talk often includes talk about women as objects, which can refer to sexual conquests and promote aggressiveness and hostility towards women. "This type of talk is not hushed," writes Curry. "Its purpose seems mainly to enhance the athletes' image of themselves to others as practicing heterosexuals" (1991, p. 128).

Here, it is also critical to note that locker room talk, with all its braggadocio, is also notoriously iffy in terms of its veracity. This discursive region invites, indeed, encourages, a heightened, exaggerated style of storytelling. As Curry writes, stories told in the locker room often "elicit knowing smiles or guffaws from the audience and it is difficult to tell whether or not they are true." The actual truth of such stories is, in this context, less important than the role the narrative plays "in buttressing the athlete's claim as a practicing heterosexual" (1991, p. 129). Stories about sexual conquests are therefore not necessarily taken at face value in the context of the locker room, which is not to say that they are not true, or do not contain some kernel of truth, but rather that the content of the story is often secondary to the masculine bonding that it affords.

Thus, to describe speech as "locker room talk" is to draw on a specific, situational understanding of truth, one that those who have previously participated in will be sure to recognize. Although the phrase does not necessarily, on its surface, imply a lack of veracity, those familiar with the nature of locker room talk may understand that this mode of speech is often exaggerated (and therefore not fully truthful). When participating in locker room talk, the conversation often shifts between fantasy and reality, and a participant who calls out a speaker, or attempts to catch a speaker in a lie, risks suffering a gaffe, as a false interpretation may constitute a breach between speaker and accuser and, further, may open the accuser up to ridicule from other members of the group (Curry, 1991, p. 132). And so within the context of the locker room, exaggerated speech, particularly speech about sexual conquests, is likely to go unchallenged, although some observers may doubt its claims.

Similarly, when men engage in exaggeration and puffing to impress and bond with one another, this may be dubbed a *bull session*. As Harry Frankfurt notes, the term *bull session* itself implies male participation (as opposed to a female, hen session), and what is distinctive about the sort of informal discussion among males, Frankfurt writes, is that "while the discussion may be intense and significant, it is in a certain respect not 'for real'" (2005, p. 35). "What tends to go on in a bull session is that the participants try out various thoughts and attitudes in order to see how it feels to hear themselves saying such things and in order to discover how others respond, without it being assumed that they are committed to what they say: it is understood by everyone in a bull session that the statements people make do not necessarily reveal what they really believe or how they really feel" (Frankfurt, 2005, p. 36). One of the most common topics of a bull session, Frankfurt notes, is sex.

Was Donald Trump aware of the link between locker room talk and less-than-truthfulness when he and his team decided to use the term as the primary discursive frame for his defense to the *Access Hollywood* tape? It is difficult to know whether this was a consideration, but one key moment from that same debate, just two days after the release of the tape, seems to suggest precisely this kind of knowing. Let us return to Trump's exchange with Anderson Cooper when pressed about his comments.

Trump:　No, I didn't say that at all. I don't think you understood what was said. This was locker-room talk. I'm not proud of it. I apologize to my family. I apologize to the American people. Certainly I'm not proud of it, but this is locker-room talk.

Trump begins his response by stating, "No, I didn't say that at all." This brief statement is, in fact, a denial. What follows, then, is a kind of explanation of the denial, in that by categorizing the speech as locker room talk, particularly in its nature and context, it can be deniable, something implicitly "unreal." But even if the audience does not believe that Trump can plausibly negate his comments in this way, they may still be swayed by his framing. Because by dubbing his words "locker room talk," Trump also expresses an implied understanding of the contextual nature, the region specificity of his speech. He therefore offers this conversational setting as a kind of explanation, asking the listener to understand and to forgive him for comments that may be perceived as indiscreet in other more public contexts.

Taken together, by characterizing his words on the *Access Hollywood* tape as *locker room* talk, Donald Trump, personally and through his surrogates, attempts to discursively self-cleave. Although he did not, at least initially, fully deny his speech on the video, Trump employed the strategic frame of *locker room talk* to distance himself from his past comments and to offer a subtle, implied denial, one which positioned his public persona as presidential candidate as distinct and separate from his private, backstage self. In doing so, Trump also insinuated that the media (a popular target of Trump's ire throughout his campaign) was, at least in part, to blame for this breach, because had his backstage comments not been brought out into the public sphere, this revelation would not have occurred.

Disavowal and Consequences

On November 9, 2016, Donald Trump was elected president of the United States. In the months to follow, Trump's face-saving approaches persisted. While on the campaign trail, Trump cleaved himself from his words on the *Access Hollywood* tape by activating the discourse of locker room talk. But once elected, these nuanced denials were replaced by explicit ones. Although, Trump initially admitted that the tape was real, according to *The New York Times*, as president-elect he "began raising the prospect with allies that it may not have been him on the tape after all" (Haberman & Martin, 2017). Reporting suggests that, in January just before the inauguration, Trump told a Republican senator that he wanted to investigate the recording, claiming that the voice on the video was not his (Haberman & Martin, 2017).

This would not be the first time Trump denied his own voice on tape. In the 1980s, Trump was reported to use a pseudonym, John Barron, "a literal alter ego that allowed him to say what he wanted, when he wanted, to the New York City press corps, and the world" (Surico, 2015). In 2016, when confronted on the *Today* show with a 14-minute audio recording of a man claiming to be Barron, Trump stated, "It was not me on the phone. . . . And it doesn't sound like me on the phone, I'll tell you that, and it was not me on the phone" (Kopan & Diamond, 2016). Although Trump's habit of posing as publicists and impersonating his own spokesperson was "an open secret" among his business associates and within NY media circles, when presented with audio evidence, he denied the sound of his own voice (Kopan & Diamond, 2016).

Could it be that Donald Trump really believed that the *Access Hollywood* tape was altered, edited, or otherwise doctored as a means of inflicting political harm? Is it possible that he truly had no recollection of his words or actions that day? As Evan Davis writes in his analysis of post-truth discourse, there is "a special category of sincerely held beliefs" where the point espoused is untrue, but where the speaker believes it to be so (2017, p. 24). But even if we believe that Trump *truly* doubts the veracity of the *Access Hollywood* tape, the outcome of his denials remains the same. The public cannot distinguish between those who are so fully taken with their own version of facts that they believe them and those who are lying intentionally. In either case, the confusion, mistrust, and ethos of doubt are perpetuated.

Trump's questionable relationship with the truth would be on full display once elected president. He repeatedly argued that he lost the popular vote in the 2016 election due to widespread voter fraud, claims that have been repeatedly debunked (Feldman, 2020; Haberman & Martin, 2017). In January 2017, White House Press Secretary Sean Spicer told reporters that the crowd at Trump's inauguration was "the largest audience to ever witness an inauguration, period, both in person and around the globe," despite the visibly smaller attendance compared to Obama's inauguration, where the audience of 1.8 million was estimated to be the most highly attended in history (Frostenson, 2017). A few days later, Counselor to the President Kellyanne Conway would appear on *Meet the Press* to defend Spicer, in an interview where she coined what would become a notorious turn of phrase, calling the comments Spicer had made "alternative facts" (Jaffe, 2017).

The list of obfuscations, insinuations, muddying statements, and outright lies that would subsequently flow from the Trump administration is too long to itemize here. So consistent and flagrant was this communication strategy that Trump would soon be dubbed the first post-truth president. Politicians have long used rhetoric and performativity to win favor and spin facts in ways that suit their political agenda, but Trump defied historical norms of expression and decorum while retaining support. It was the audience's reaction to, and belief in, Trump's performance that served as a barometer of his success, not the veracity of his words.

And it is precisely this foregrounding of perception over reality that political theorist Shannon Bow O'Brien notes in her (2020) book *Donald Trump and the Kayfabe Presidency*. O'Brien contends that, in order to understand the politics of Trump, one must return to the world of professional wrestling. It is this forum, with its commitment to kayfabe, that defines not only Trump's personal ethos but his political brand and the machinations of his presidential administration. O'Brien argues that Trump so vigorously maintained kayfabe as president that his public performance of manufactured reality allowed him to behave outrageously while deflecting criticism (2020, p. 4). Trump's White House functioned as an enclosed bubble, in which the president and his allies' opinions were the only valid and acceptable ones, where truth was rooted in the emphaticness of the administration's assertions rather than in concrete facts, and where any contradictions, no matter how clear or well-documented, were deemed irrelevant (2020, p. 31).

Trump encouraged his supporters to revel in the showmanship of his speeches, the spectacle of the fights (there was a new one every day), and the antagonism of his opponents; his base responded in kind, and all political conventions that sought to separate spectacle and governance were wiped away (2020, p. 53). In the world of kayfabe, backtracking, apologizing, and clarifying are signs of weakness; meaning is absolute, and concessions are not allowed (O'Brien, 2020, p. 90). Trump's use of aggressive, hostile language throughout his tenure as president worked to create and enhance political and cultural in and out groups, and then pit members of those groups against one another in ways that mirrored the battles for good and evil enacted in the wrestling ring. Trump's followers heard the message and understood the rules of the match. Many became more and more ardent in their support, since knowing the truth meant hearing it directly from Trump (Lawler, 2023). They would fight to the death and cheer their victor, regardless of the circumstances.

We can see the operationalization of kayfabe in Trump's use of the term *fake news*, a turn of phrase he would use so often that it would become inextricably linked to his presidency. *Fake news* is a term intended to cast doubt not only on the specific truth claim but also on the information environment wholesale. When faced with news reports, journalists, opinions, or people he did not like or disagreed with, Trump dubbed them *fake news*, a convenient and expeditious way of dismissing the offender. No further explanation required. *Fake news* is, in this way, both a label and a tactic. *Fake news* diminishes the value of the target, story, or opinion to which it is applied. At the same time, it also suggests that there is a high volume of misinformation circulating in the information environment, and that we the audience should be in a constant state of vigilance, on the lookout for imposters and frauds. Thus, *fake news* is not only a defense against those whose ideas or position might contradict one's own but also a tool for encouraging public skepticism, prompting us to be on guard against any persons or pieces of information that may conflict with our own worldview. *Fake news* is satisfying, to that end, because it gives permission to accept only that which confirms our previously existing beliefs and assumptions, regardless of their provability. Although politicians have long attempted to allude to inconvenient points about the careers and polices, Trump's use of fake news exaggerated that practice through the normalization of repeated lies and denials and the casual use of blatant falsehood as a tool of public address (Corner, 2017, p. 1101).

What are the consequences when self-cleaving discourses are employed by a powerful actor, willing to distort and manipulate in order to continuously bolster his own political capital? First, the implications for civil society are clear. Trump has broken traditions of American political decorum, once taken for granted, and in doing so, opened the door for a confrontational, hyperpartisan style of governing, based not on policy positions (recall how the GOP dispensed with a party platform in 2020; their message was, simply, Trump [Epstein, 2020]) or broader political goal setting but on personal branding, convenience, and opportunism, epitomized by the recent rise of political figures like Matt Gaetz, Marjorie Taylor Greene, and George Santos (Blake, 2023). In this political model, the personality of the leader prevails over all else. It is the sole source of truth and the guiding force. Taken to an extreme, it is a cult of personality in which the leader becomes an idol (Tharoor, 2022). In such an environment, fact is evanescent and conspiracy theories thrive.

The most damning outcome of this turn is evidenced in the January 6, 2021, attack on the US capitol, during which rioters, spurred by an erroneous belief that Trump had won the 2020 election, enacted their rage on government personnel and infrastructure. The political violence that ensued was sparked by lies, and it resulted in destruction, mayhem, and death. This tragedy also demonstrates a breakdown in public trust, a doubt of citizen's faith in their own free-and-fair elections, and a severely polarized political landscape in which belief systems are so divided as to be fundamentally incompatible, so that dialogue and cooperation are replaced by violence.

In this milieu, mainstream news media and journalism have faced critical questions about how to report factual information. Many journalists have attempted to manage Trump's contradictory statements and lies by pointing out their flaws or attempting to expose them as incorrect. Others, in a grasp at neutrality, attempted to show "both sides" of an issue. These strategies, however well-intentioned, have done little to undermine Trump's position or popularity, because they both fundamentally serve to further publicize his rhetoric and claims (Ball, 2017). As journalist James Ball writes in his analysis of post-truth media, Trump's strategies bind us in a trap: "Superficially at least – bullshit works: if challenged, it provokes a story about the row that repeats the claim for days at a time; if unchallenged, the claim seems unanswerable" (Ball, 2017, p. 5). Plus, this constant churn drives ratings, incentivizing media attention on the most dramatic, outrageous, and salacious stories. As CBS chief executive Les Moonves commented in 2016, the spectacle of the Trump administration "may not be good for America, but it's damn good for CBS. . . . The money's rolling in, and this is fun" (Bond, 2016).

Media attention is partially responsible for Trump's 2016 election; during his campaign, the candidate earned nearly $2 billion in free media coverage – much more than any candidate in recent memory – thanks to his outlandish statements and penchant for controversy. This backdoor financial windfall allowed him to sidestep the traditional fundraising model of presidential politics (Confessore & Yourish, 2016). But news media has also paid a hefty price for its inability to grapple with Trump's antics without further promoting them. Public trust in journalism, already in decline, fell off sharply during Trump's tenure as president. According to Pew Research Center, the percentage of adults who say they trust mainstream news media decreased by 18 points, down to 58% overall, and 35% among Republicans, between 2016 and 2021 (2021). This lack of public faith in journalism perpetuates an information environment in which speculation and conspiracy theories can easily multiply, further driving misinformation and preventing citizens from engaging in informed debate.

To be sure, Trump's self-cleaving rhetoric was just one part of a broader media campaign of obfuscation, denials, and outright lies. Yet we can understand self-cleaving as a critical touchstone, a key image management strategy that helps to explain the form and function of Trump's speech as it relates to his presentation of self and claims on authenticity and "realness." When this strategy is activated by the leader of the US government and military, we see the direct and immediate impacts: public trust in institutions and journalism declines, polarization among the electorate is heightened (Durham, 2022), and our ability to discern fact from fiction is tested. Even now that Trump is no longer in office, 71% of his supporters believe what he says is true, more so than they believe friends, family, conservative media figures, or religious leaders (Lawler, 2023).

As Tamar Liebes writes in her (2001) analysis, a consideration of Trump's political self-presentation recalls one of the landmark studies of early radio. In 1946, Robert Merton published a study of the famous singer Kate Smith's hugely successful on-air war bond sales campaign in which he describes the singer's address to listeners as one which was compelling because it spoke "to them," directly addressing each person, as an individual, using interpersonal markers of sincerity. Merton calls this kind of media talk "pseudo-gemeinschaft" and notes its potential to foster a feigned feeling of social connection, one that cunningly activates a feeling of personal concern with others to manipulate them all the more effectively (Merton, 1946, p. 142). Particularly in moments of national strife – whether it be the Second World War or the Covid-19 pandemic – the public views sincerity as a reassuring balm and citizens may seek politicians who are perceived as being sincere (Liebes, 2001). Yet, as Liebes points out, our fear of being manipulated by politicians who are perceived as self-motivated or phony may lead us to crave sincerity so much so that we fail to notice the ways in which this, too, may be a contrivance, a media conjuring trick (Liebes, 2001, p. 503).

In addition, the political elevation of a man who used his power and managed his image in ways to obfuscate, excuse, and otherwise enable his own misogynistic remarks and predatory actions revealed an unsettling truth about sexism and rape culture in contemporary America (Durham, 2022). Despite gains in education, professional opportunities, and gender representation in Congress, women could still be objectified, harassed, and assaulted with impunity by powerful men, whose cultural or political capital would not be harmed (and might even be enhanced) by their behaviors. As Meenakshi Gigi Durham writes, the fact that Trump was elected president – his self-cleaving strategies seemingly successful – demonstrated to American women that "a misogynistic belief system can be institutionally entrenched, supported, and rewarded by the political apparatus at national levels" and that rape culture is "an officially sanctioned and institutionally protected social phenomenon" (2022, p. 53). Further, studies suggest that exposure to peers (and consequently, future presidents) who verbally sexually objectify and disrespect women, as in the case of "locker room talk," decreases the likelihood of prosocial bystander intervention and heightens men's adherence to hegemonic norms of masculinity (Leonne & Parrott, 2019). For the next four years, Americans would be exposed to a national leader whose words and actions modeled precisely this type of behavior.

Faced with this stark realization, women worldwide organized, spoke out on social media, and took to the streets. The January 21, 2017, Women's March, which took place the day after Trump's inauguration, served as cultural reckoning. Women in cities across the world rallied in protest; many donned pink "pussy hats" and toted signs that referenced Trump's *Access Hollywood* comments. The march was likely the largest single-day demonstration in US history, with approximately four million people, more than 1% of the nation's population, taking part (Chenoweth & Pressman, 2017). By October of Trump's first year in office, #MeToo would become a viral hashtag, with millions of women sharing their stories of sexual assault, abuse, and violence on social media. The strength of #MeToo during this period can be understood as a response to emergent public revelations about the alleged abuses of powerful and highly visible men, including Donald Trump. The surging visibility and influence of the #MeToo movement during Trump's presidency suggest that although media platforms had played a critical role in elevating Trump to national office, these technologies could also be effective tools for those seeking to speak out, organize, reject misogyny, and stake their own claims on the value of truth.

Notes

1 I accessed and transcribed all portions of the *Access Hollywood* video quoted in this document using *The Washington Post* video channel. Although the video is now widely available through a variety of online sources, I chose *TWP* channel since it was the *Post*'s reporting that originally broke the story. All quotations are transcriptions that I created using the audio in the clips and did not rely on the closed captions provided by the network. At the time of publication, the video can be accessed here. https://www.washingtonpost.com/video/national/watch-donald-trump-recorded-having-extremely-lewd-conversation-about-women-in-2005/2016/10/07/3bf16d1e-8caf-11e6-8cdc-4fbb1973b506_video.html

2 Reports suggest that, upon first hearing the tape on October 7th, Trump remarked, "This doesn't sound like me"; however, upon seeing the video, he then said, "Well, that's me." Campaign manager Kellyanne Conway told reporters, "He legitimately did not remember saying that" (Alberta, 2019).

References

ABC. (2016, September 16). How Donald Trump perpetuated the "birther" movement for years. *ABC News*.

Alberta, T. (2019, July 10). "Mother is not going to like this": The 48 hours that almost brought down Trump. The exclusive story of how Trump survived the "Access Hollywood" tape. *Politico*.

Ball, J. (2017). *Post-truth: How bullshit conquered the world*. Biteback Publishing.

Barbaro, M., & Twohey, M. (2016, May 14). Crossing the line: How Donald Trump behaved with women in private. *The New York Times*.

Ben-Zeev, A., Scharnetzki, L., Chan, L. K., & Dennehy, T. C. (2012). Hyper-masculinity in the media: When men "walk into the fog" to avoid affective communication. *Psychology of Popular Media Culture, 1*(1), 53–61.

Blake, A. (2023, January 18). The stark irony of George Santos's and Marjorie Taylor Greene's committees. *The Washington Post*.

Bond, P. (2016, February 29). Leslie Moonves on Donald Trump: "It may not be good for America, but it's damn good for CBS". *The Hollywood Reporter*.

Cassidy, B. (2019, May 10). Donald Trump's business failures were very real. *The New Yorker*.

Chenoweth, E., & Pressman, J. (2017, February 7). This is what we learned by counting the women's marches. *The Washington Post*.

Confessore, N., & Yourish, K. (2016, March 15). $2 billion worth of free media for Donald Trump. *The New York Times*.

Corner, J. (2017). Fake news, post-truth and media political change. *Media, Culture & Society, 39*(7), 1100–1107.

Curry, T. J. (1991). Fraternal bonding in the locker room: A profeminist analysis of talk about competition and women. *Sociology of Sport Journal, 8*(2), 119–135.

Darnell, S. C., & Wilson, B. (2006). Macho media: Unapologetic hypermasculinity in Vancouver's "talk radio for guys". *Journal of Broadcasting and Electronic Media, 50*(3), 444–466.

Davis, E. (2017). *Post-truth: Why we have reached peak bullshit and what we can do about it.* Little, Brown.

Dawsey, J. (2017, January 16). Trump's obsession with WrestleMania and fake drama. *Politico.*

Durham, M. G. (2022). *MeToo: The impact of rape culture in the media.* Polity.

Epstein, R. J. (2020, August 25). The G.O.P. delivers its political platform: It's from 2016. *The New York Times.*

Fahrenthold, D. (2016, October 8). Trump recorded having extremely lewd conversation about women in 2005. *The Washington Post.*

Feldman, M. (2020, May 27). *10 voter fraud lies debunked.* The Brennan Center for Justice.

Fleishman, J. (2016, October 14). Trump's "Access Hollywood" unmasking and the searing power of video to shape the historic moment. *Los Angeles Times.*

Frankfurt, H. (2005). *On bullshit.* Princeton University Press.

Frostenson, S. (2017, January 24). A crowd scientist says Trump's inauguration attendance was pretty average. *Vox.*

Goffman, E. (1959). *The presentation of self in everyday life.* Anchor Books.

Goffman, E. (1967). *Interaction ritual.* Doubleday.

Graham, D. A. (2016, October 7). Trump brags about groping women. *The Atlantic.*

Grant, J. (1996). Bring the noise: Hypermasculinity in heavy metal and rap. *Journal of Social Philosophy, 27*(2), 5–31.

Haberman, M., & Martin, J. (2017, November 28). Trump once said the "Access Hollywood" tape was real: Now he's not sure. *The New York Times.*

Jaffe, A. (2017, January 22). Kellyanne Conway: WH spokesman gave "alternative facts" on inauguration crowd. *NBC News.*

Jimerson, J. J. (2001). A conversation (re)analysis of fraternal bonding in the locker room. *Sociology of Sport Journal, 18*(3), 317–338.

Johnston, I. (2016, October 7). Trump claims Bill Clinton said "far worse to me" amid storm over lewd remarks about women. *The Independent.*

Keneally, M. (2017, November 27). What Trump previously said about the 2005 "Access Hollywood" tape that he's now questioning. *ABC News.*

Kopan, T., & Diamond, J. (2016, May 14). Donald Trump on recording: Not me. *CNN.*

Lawler, D. (2023, August 21). Trump voters trust him more than their families, religious leaders: Poll. *Axios.*

Leonne, R. M., & Parrott, D. J. (2019). Misogynistic peers, masculinity, and bystander intervention for sexual aggression: Is it really just "locker-room talk?" *Aggressive Behavior, 45*, 42–51.

Liebes, T. (2001). "Look me straight in the eye": The political discourse of authenticity, spontaneity, and sincerity. *The Communication Review, 4*, 499–510.

Majors, Y. (2003). Shoptalk: Teaching and learning in an African American hair salon. *Mind, Culture, and Activity*, *10*(4), 289–310.

McDonnell, A., & Wheeler, M. (2019). @realDonaldTrump: Political celebrity, authenticity, and para-social engagement on Twitter. *Celebrity Studies*, *10*(3), 427–431.

Merton, R. (1946). *Mass persuasion: The social psychology of a war bond drive*. Harper & Bros.

Montgomery, M. (2017). Post-truth politics? Authenticity, populism and the electoral discourses of Donald Trump. *Journal of Language and Politics*, *16*(4), 619–639.

Montgomery, M., Higgins, M., & Smith, A. (2019). Political offensiveness in the mediated public sphere: The performative play of alignments. In A. Graefer (Ed.), *Media and the politics of offence*. Palgrave.

Newport, F., & Saad, L. (2016, March 4). Trump support built on outsider status, business experience. *Gallup*. Retrieved November 6, 2023, from https://news.gallup.com/poll/189773/trump-support-built-outsider-status-business-experience.aspx

O'Brien, S. B. (2020). *Donald Trump and the kayfabe presidency: Professional wrestling in the White House*. Palgrave.

Peterson-Withorn, C. (2016, March 31). How Donald Trump exaggerates and fibs about his $4.5 billion net worth. *Forbes*.

Pew Research Center. (2021, August 30). *Wider partisan gaps emerge in trust of national and local news organizations, social media*. Retrieved December 2, 2023, from https://www.pewresearch.org/short-reads/2021/08/30/partisan-divides-in-media-trust-widen-driven-by-a-decline-among-republicans/

Phelps, J., Siegel, B., & Abramson, A. (2016, October 8). McCain joins growing ranks of Republicans withdrawing support for Trump. *ABC News*.

Poniewozik, J. (2019, September 6). The real Donald Trump is a character on TV. *The New York Times*.

Radden Keefe, P. (2018, December 27). How Mark Burnett resurrected Donald Trump as an icon of American success. *New Yorker*.

Rhodes, J. H., Sharrow, E. A., Greenlee, J. S., & Nteta, T. M. (2020). Just locker room talk? Explicit sexism and the impact of the "Access Hollywood" tape on electoral support for Donald Trump in 2016. *Political Communication*, *37*(6).

Roy, J. (2016, March 15). Trump spokesperson says it was his TV character, not him, who made all those sexist comments. *The Cut*.

Scannell, P. (1996). *Radio, television, and modern life: A phenomenological approach*. Wiley.

Sewer, A. (2020, May 13). Birtherism of a nation. *The Atlantic*.

Snyder, J., & Clerkin, A. (2016, October 5). Exclusive: One-on-one with presidential candidate Donald Trump. *ABC 3 News*.

Spender, D. (1980). *Man made language*. Routledge.

Surico, J. (2015, November 6). Remembering John Barron: Donald Trump's "spokesman" alter ego. *Vice*. Retrieved December 19, 2023, from https://web.archive.org/web/20180613184422/https://www.vice.com/en_us/article/exqkbp/remembering-john-barron-donald-trumps-spokesman-alter-ego-116

Tharoor, I. (2022, August 19). Trump's personality cult and the erosion of U.S. democracy. *The Washington Post.*

Trump, D. J. (2000, February 19). What I saw at the revolution. *The New York Times*, *A*, p. B15.

Vaynman, M. J., Sandberg, S., & Pedersen, W. (2020). "Locker room talk": Male bonding and sexual degradation in drinking stories. *Culture, Health & Sexuality*, *22*(11), 1235–1252.

Waxman, O. B. (2019, May 31). President Trump played a key role in the central park five case. Here's the real history behind "when they see us". *Time.*

3 R. Kelly // Robert Kelly

If you turned on the radio in the 1990s or early 2000s, chances are good that you would soon hear an R. Kelly song. The R&B artist rose to the top of the charts with a string of hits, including *Ignition, Bump n' Grind*, and *I Believe I Can Fly*, which were notable not only for their popularity but also for their crossover appeal. Kelly's songs were hits with a hip-hop audience and a mainstream pop base; they could be danced to at the club and sung at gospel concerts. Tragically, however, the duality of Kelly's musical abilities was also reflected in his behavior and self-image. While his inspirational songs and charismatic persona allowed Kelly to present as a successful and aspirational figure, particularly in the Black community, they also provided a cover for predatory behavior that, it would eventually become clear, he was engaging for years. Meanwhile, his raunchier songs and sexual lyrics allowed Kelly to occupy what journalist Ann Powers calls "a position of outrageousness," a public image that blended and blurred a hypersexual musical persona with real-life predation of the vulnerable (hampton, 2019). Kelly also benefited from the intersections of racial and gendered credibility gaps that disproportionately affected his victims, activating stereotypes about the assumed promiscuousness of Black women and girls.

Kelly's position of outrageousness rests on a long-standing practice of discursive self-cleaving, a strategy which successfully shielded him from punishment for years. And yet, in time, the flagrancy of Kelly's crimes, combined with social change stemming from the #MeToo and #MuteRKelly movements, ultimately resulted in his facing significant professional and legal consequences. This chapter documents Kelly's use of discursive self-cleaving to simultaneously perform inspirational and debased personas, the apparent contradictions of which blurred together to create a smokescreen, obscuring the "real" R. Kelly and the real depth of his crimes. These tensions clearly emerge in Kelly's 2019 CBS interview with Gayle King.[1] By attending to Kelly's rhetoric in that interview, we can observe his self-articulated positioning as he explains it during a moment in which it is breaking down. Finally, whereas the previous two chapters have explored cases in which self-cleaving practices have proved, to date, successful in circumventing legal and practical consequences, Kelly's self-cleaving ultimately failed to prevent him from facing repercussions for

DOI: 10.4324/9781003380139-4

his actions. Indeed, his last grasps at the dual persona to which he had so desperately clung revealed self-cleaving as the farcical machinations of a criminal, prompting parody and ridicule in the mainstream media. Why did Kelly's self-cleaving ultimately fail? What role did race play in both sustaining and unraveling Kelly's image? And how can we understand the influence of social movements, especially those led by Black women, in bringing Kelly's crimes to light?

Creating and Occupying a Position of Outrageousness

Throughout the 1990s, R. Kelly became a household name, selling 75 million records worldwide, establishing himself as one of the most commercially successful R&B artists of the era, and producing a string of hits including *Ignition* and *Step in the Name of Love* (Billboard). In 1994, his song *Bump n' Grind* brought Kelly's sexuality to the forefront of popular music. The song rocketed to number one on the Billboard Hot 100 chart and remained there for four weeks (Breihan, 2022). But while his discography often featured overt, graphically sexual lyrics and his stage shows included displays that an observer would later describe as "increasingly pornographic," Kelly also gained mainstream success with uplifting, gospel-inspired music that appealed to a wider audience (hampton, 2019). In the mid-1990s, *I Believe I Can Fly* became a blockbuster single, winning four Grammy awards. The theme song for the 1996 film *Space Jam*, which featured basketball heroes Michael Jordan and Larry Bird alongside an animated cast of Looney Toon characters, *IBICF* brought Kelly into the mainstream of American media culture while endearing him to children, parents, members of the gospel community, and others who may have found his raunchier content less palatable (hampton, 2019).

It was this string of successes that helped shift public attention away from some of the more suspicious behaviors in which Kelly was engaged. In the early 1990s, Kelly had begun grooming Aaliyah, a talented, 12-year-old R&B performer, appearing with her in media interviews, where he coyly dodged questions about their relationship (Grady, 2021). Aaliyah's first hit song, produced by Kelly, was titled "Age Ain't Nothing but a Number." The song, in which a younger girl sings about seducing an older man, featured lyrics like "I don't mean to be bold, but I gotta let you know, I gotta thang for you and I can't let go. . . . Boy be brave, don't be afraid, cause tonight we're gonna go all the way." Given the highly visible relationship between Kelly and Aaliyah at the time, this song could have been viewed as a danger sign. But Kelly skillfully used it to toy with public perception, cloaking his actions in the creativity of his professional talents and evading sustained scrutiny (Tsioulcas, 2021).

A 27-year-old Kelly illegally married Aaliyah in 1994, bribing an Illinois government official to obtain a fake ID and listing Aaliyah's age as 18 on the marriage license – she was actually 15 at the time (Hong, 2019). The marriage was later annulled (Grady, 2021). In December that same year, rumors swirled that Kelly had married Aaliyah so that he could legally provide her permission to obtain an abortion, as she had allegedly become pregnant with his child. *Vibe* published the marriage certificate, and what was once off-color industry speculation became a matter of public record (Grady, 2021).

But that did not temper Kelly's behavior, and in the years to follow, both Kelly's activities and the rumors about him continued to escalate. In 1995, Kelly released "Down Low," a song that describes meeting a college-aged girl and locking the doors while "that silly bitch is screaming rape." In 2000, the *Chicago Sun Times* reported that Kelly was using his fame to meet and pursue sexual relations with girls as young as 15 (Arkin, 2021). The following year, speculation about Kelly's interest in minors received renewed attention when a former Epic Records intern, Tracy Sampson, filed a lawsuit against Kelly in which she alleged that the singer had coerced her into a sexual relationship with him when she was 17 (Cush, 2019). Around this same time, a video surfaced and began circulating throughout the Chicago area, appearing to depict Kelly having sex with – and urinating on – a young girl. The existence of the video was reported by the *Sun Times* in February 2002, after an anonymous tipster sent a copy to the paper (Arkin, 2021). Months later, Kelly was indicted in Chicago on child pornography charges related to the tape; court filings would allege that the victim was 14 years old at the time the film was created.

While these charges were pending, Kelly released the sprawling concept album *Trapped in the Closet* (2005). Part confessional, part soap opera, part parody, the album features 22 songs ("chapters") with accompanying music videos and a range of characters, including pimps, gangsters, and prostitutes. The protagonist Sylvester (Kelly's middle name) is played by the singer himself, and he sings the plot, which revolves around a man who wakes up after a one-night stand with a woman and then, confronted by her husband, is forced to hide in a closet. The lyrics include explicit references to domestic abuse and physical violence, including "Ya better start talkin, bitch 'fore I take a match and burn this muthaf*cka down" and "baby you gone be breathless if ya don't start talkin quick. Woman, I'm gone have a fit. You don't know what ya f*ckin with." Released at a pivotal moment in Kelly's legal proceedings, *Trapped in the Closet* reached #22 on the US charts, and the music videos, available for online streaming, obtained a cult following (Petridis, 2007). Notably, the album's over-the-top drama and soapy, campy presentation gave audiences and critics the ability to laugh at, and perhaps along with, Kelly, to feel as if we were in on a kind of joke about him and his sex life, precisely at a moment when Kelly was facing grave charges. *Trapped in the Closet* also showcased Kelly performing himself as a character, Sylvester, and taking on this role by way of enacting elements of his real life vicariously through a fictional persona. In this moment, we see Kelly begin to try on multiple selves and to test the potential benefits of self-cleaving as they relate to his own image management.

It would take six years for the child pornography case to come to trial, but in 2008, a Chicago jury found R. Kelly not guilty of 21 counts related to the production of the sex tape. During this legal delay, 12 additional charges related to the alleged production of pornography were brought, and dropped (Savage, 2023). Had R. Kelly been vindicated? Or had he simply managed to use his fame and influence to evade justice? Either way, the music industry and mainstream media were ready to move on. Accusations against Kelly were made the butt of the joke, with comedian Dave Chappelle and the popular animated series *South Park* parodying the allegations for laughs. Little attention was paid to the harm Kelly had allegedly done to his victims. Few publicly worried over the possibility that an acquittal could perpetuate his ability to abuse others (Tsioulcas, 2021).

Kelly's post-trial activities suggested that the verdict had liberated him from fear of retribution for his actions. His lyrics, performances, and public behavior became even more sexualized and confrontational. Kelly took to calling himself "the Pied Piper of R&B" (Heath, 2016), a moniker which references the story of a musician who leads a group of children away from their homes never to be seen again. When journalists suggested that this nickname might be problematic, an insensitive and worrying choice given the charges of sexual predation of minors leveled against him, Kelly brushed them aside, telling *GQ* magazine, "You know, I can't believe that people really think deeply like that."

It's kind of jokey to me, it's goofy, because I don't think enough people think that deep into me, they would compare me to some man that leads children out of the community and kills them. There's no way they would buy my albums, there would be no way they would come to my concerts – anybody that thinks that way is sick. So definitely can't pay them no time.

(Heath, 2016)

In this statement, Kelly points to his professional success as form of self-defense, one which uses the public's support of him as supposed evidence of his good nature. The radio host Charlamagne the God describes Kelly's use of such an overt nickname, a "middle finger," a way of parading his untouchability (hampton, 2019, Episode 6).

Over the next decade, Kelly remained a popular and profitable celebrity and hit maker, producing new music and solidifying his status as a local hero in Chicago neighborhoods, where he had grown up and continued to frequent. He would also continue to abuse – mostly Black – young women and girls. In the months and years to follow, dozens of women came forward to accuse Kelly of sexual violence, coercion, kidnapping, and abuse (Cush, 2019). Eventually, Kelly was back in court, facing two federal trials involving allegations of abuse against 11 girls and women, having taken place over the course of more than 20 years (Tsioulcas, 2021). He was first convicted in New York in 2021 on charges of federal racketeering and sex trafficking, for which he is serving a 30-year sentence. The following year, he was found guilty of an additional six counts of sexual exploitation and enticement of a minor (Sammee Ali, 2022). But while these verdicts may have afforded Kelly's victims some modicum of justice, they also prompted many to ask one critical question: How could Kelly have possibly gotten away with this behavior for so long?

R. Kelly's catalog of graphically sexual music and uplifting songs of inspiration, combined with his use of humor and savvy manipulation of the press, produced a cleaved dual persona consisting of inspirational and debased selves. In the 2019 documentary series by dream hampton *Surviving R. Kelly (SRK)*, Ann Powers describes how these competing personas were mutually beneficial in providing Kelly cover for his crimes, allowing him to "hide in plain sight" for more than a decade. Kelly's inspirational self was cultivated through "good works, good music, music that is uplifting and transcendent . . . inspirational songs and his . . . gospel side." This inspirational persona allowed him to maintain a widely popular and palatable image, even as the seriousness of the allegations against him continued to mount. At the same time, Kelly cultivated a debased persona, creating outrageous art, "embodying the very stereotype that [his] private life seems to fulfill," crafting and occupying "a position of outrageousness" through obscene songs about explicit sex acts that "masked everything that was happening behind the scenes" (hampton, 2019, Episode 2). This debased persona allowed Kelly to openly flaunt his sexual predilections and criminal ideations under the guise of artistry and then explain those actions away, accusing anyone who questioned him as being a prudish hater, a stiff who couldn't discern the difference between entertainment and reality.

Kelly's discursive self-cleaving presents both an inspirational and a debased version of himself and then dares the audience to accuse him of being the latter. The presence of the inspirational Kelly functions as a psychological point of dissonance for the audience. We ask ourselves, how can the allegations against Kelly be true when he has made music that has been so uplifting? The debased Kelly then capitalizes on that seed of doubt, engaging in increasingly flagrant behaviors, producing more sexually and violently graphic music, and insisting that these, too, are merely performances. His work, as Nelson George notes in *SRK*, is "very much telling on itself. . . . Throughout his music, he's been remarkably frank about his predilections, about his freakiness, about levels of control" (hampton, 2019, Episode 6). As clinical psychologist Dr. Jody Adewale notes, "oftentimes, perpetrators will be so brave to say, 'I'm gonna let the world know. I'm gonna let everyone see what's going on, and you'd better not say anything'" (hampton, 2019, Episode 1).

This progressively daring image management mirrors, on a mass-mediated scale, the type of psychological grooming that abusers like Kelly often use on their victims. Intimate partner violence does not only involve physical or sexual abuse but also includes psychological manipulation and emotional abuse aimed at coercion and control (CDC, 2022). According to the National Domestic

Violence Hotline, gaslighting, in which an abuser prompts others to doubt their own observations and experiences, is a common feature of emotional abuse (NDVH, 2023). Gaslighting may involve one partner making the other feel confused or "crazy" by withholding information, claiming to forget or deny past events, or trivializing concerns. Gaslighting shares features in common with a post-truth information economy, in that it uses counternarratives, discreditation, and denial of plain facts, to leave observers feeling disoriented while eroding our sense of self-trust to consolidate the rhetorical and actual power of the speaker (Rietdijk, 2021).

In *SRK*, many of the women Kelly targeted and abused describe in clear and harrowing detail the way in which Kelly used precisely this type of emotional abuse to groom them, often from a young age. Andrea Kelly, R. Kelly's ex-wife who met him at the age of 19, says she fell in love with a "charmer" but that, over time, another person crept in who made her doubt her own sense of judgment. But because she remembered the man she originally cared for, she described a time when she adapted her own behaviors to "get him back to the good guy, the one that I fell in love with" (hampton, 2019, Episode 2). Indeed, numerous women who describe their experiences in *SRK* explicitly reference Kelly's cleaved selves, describing R. Kelly as a fun-loving, sweet guy, and Robert as "the devil."

In March 2019, just two weeks after he was arrested and charged with ten counts of aggravated sexual abuse, and two months after *Lifetime* aired the six-part *Surviving R. Kelly* documentary series, bringing survivors' stories into the national spotlight, Kelly sat down for a television interview with Gayle King for CBS's *This Morning*. What follows is an analysis of Kelly's discourse during this interview, which is notable because it occurs during a time in which his image was in crisis and under serious legal and public relations threat.

During the conversation, King directly asks Kelly about his cleaved selves and whether he has a split personality, and Kelly goes on to explain how he sees himself in his own words:

King: This is what I hear
Kelly: Ok.
King: That there's a difference between R. Kelly, the entertainer, and Robert Kelly, the man. You know where I'm going with that.
Kelly: Oh no, I don't know where you're going. I just said
King: One is charming and likable. One is very controlling and abusive. That's where I'm going with that.
Kelly: Is that a rumor?
King: Are there two R Kelly's? There's a Robert and there's an R. Kelly.
Kelly: Like Dr. Jekyll and Mr. Hyde.
King: All right. We'll go with that.
Kelly: Absolutely not. Absolutely not.
King: Ok.

Initially, Kelly denies the existence of a cleaved self; however, he then refers to the classic story of Dr. Jekyll and Mr. Hyde, whose titular characters are two halves of a cleaved self: the former, a respected scientist who develops a potion that allows him to separate the good and evil aspects of his personality and to transform into the later, an evil, unrepentant alter-ego. Kelly then elaborates on this concept, providing additional detail about his self-view:

Kelly: Robert is the guy who sings. His singing name is R. Kelly. It's equivalent to a policeman.

King: Yes.

Kelly: When a policeman put on his badge and his suit and his uniform, he go out to do his job. When he take that uni- When he's on that job, he's a beast, he's tough, he has to be. He's got to be in control. He's got to be, not out of control. You gotta do his work. When he takes that off and gets home, he's with his family. He loves his family. And if he's single, he may mingle, but however, he's still here to serve and protect at the time he's told to do it. I'm R. Kelly on stage, okay, but that's Robert in an R. Kelly uniform.

Kelly's comments provide a first-person assessment of his own self-cleaving. Here, we see Kelly making two key rhetorical moves. First, he describes his stage persona as a uniform, or a costume, something that he puts on to do his job and perform in the public sphere. When in uniform, Kelly suggests, he occupies a distinct role, one in which certain elements of his personality are heightened, namely his need to be "tough," "a beast," and "in control." When he reenters the private, domestic sphere of the home and family, he says that he removes that costume and reveals the Robert underneath. This description echoes the argument made by Terry Bollea when describing his public and private versions of self. Kelly's account of his on-stage uniform bolsters his previous claims that his hypersexual performances and hypermasculine behavior are simply elements of his act, not indicative of his "real" life.

But as Kelly develops the uniform analogy further, the distinction between these cleaved selves begins to unravel. He notes that his uniform is not something that is ever fully put away; it is always at the ready, suggesting that he can slip between roles easily and at any time. And Kelly concludes with a statement that, in its frankness, reveals something about his cleaved selves that is much closer to the truth. He tells King that his stage persona is "Robert in an R. Kelly uniform," and while that statement is, in and of itself, consistent with his explanation to this point, it marks a rhetorical shift in that it emphasizes not the difference between these two selves but the sameness. The backstage and the frontstage performances, to use Goffman's (1956) framework, may be different, but the performer who occupies those spaces is the same person.

Weaponized Belligerence

The *CBS* interview between King and Kelly took place over more than 80 minutes, and, when it aired during a primetime special on March 8, 2019, it was edited for clarity, interspersed with video footage explaining the long-standing allegations against Kelly, and was not broadcast in its entirety. The interview was the most-watched show of that evening, drawing 6.6 million viewers (Haring, 2019). By attending to key portions of the interview, we can observe the strategies Kelly used to self-cleave within the discursive space of the exchange, and how he activated the two-sides of his inspirational-debased image in turns to deflect the allegations against him and present himself as the true victim. We also see how Kelly weaponized belligerence to distract while gaslighting the audience, prompting us to doubt our own factual understanding of the case.

The interview is staged with King and Kelly seated directly across from one another. Throughout, a variety of camera angles, both establishing and close-up, show the participants' body language and facial expressions. King opens one pivotal exchange by asking Kelly what he wants to communicate through the interview:

King: I am surprised that you agreed to do it. Why are you sitting down with us today?

Kelly: I'm very tired of all the lies. I've been hearing things you know and seeing things on the blogs and you know. I'm just tired.

King: What are the lies that you're hearing that disturb you most?

Kelly: Oh my god. All of 'em. That little girl is trapped in a basement. Helicopters over my house trying to rescue someone that doesn't need rescuing because they're not in my house. Handcuffing people. Starving people. I have a harem, whatcha call it, a cult.

King: Mmmhmm.

Kelly: I don't really know what a cult is, but I know I don't have one.

King: Have you done anything that you regret? Have you done anything wrong?

Kelly: Lots of things wrong when it comes to women that I apologize, but I apologize in those relationships at the time I was in the relationships.

King: Have you broken any laws when it comes to women?

Kelly: Absolutely not.

Initially, Kelly offers a complete denial of wrongdoing. He describes and acknowledges the claims against him but notes that he is "disturbed" by allegations of his abuse. He also recognizes mistakes he has previously made but limits those apologies to actions that took place first, in the past, and second, in the private sphere of his personal life. The interview continues with King asking Kelly about the recently released *Surviving R. Kelly* documentary and the allegations contained therein:

King: The six-part series [*SRK*] interviewed 50 people
Kelly: Mmmhmm.
King: Family members, your former tour manager, numerous women who all claim you abused them. Are you saying that everybody in that documentary was not telling the truth about you? Everybody?
Kelly: If you really look at that documentary, which I'm sure you have
King: I have.
Kelly: Everybody says something bad about me. Nobody said nothing good. They was describing Lucifer. I'm not Lucifer. I'm a man. I make mistakes but I'm not a devil and by no means am I a monster.

Here, Kelly uses the specters of the devil and monsters to draw a distinction between his "real," human self and a fantastical, evil self. Kelly's use of this language mirrors that of his accusers in *SRK* – women do in fact describe him as a "monster" – but Kelly's choice to use these words should not be understood as an echoing of survivors' voices. Rather, he uses this language as a rhetorical cue, linking claims against him to the realm of fantasy and, in doing so, suggesting that these accusations are not based in the world of reality (i.e. the human world). At the same time, Kelly's language alludes to the long-standing media discourse around his debased persona and his claims that his is merely a performative public image, not indicative of his true self.

The interview continues, as King recites the names of women who spoke out against Kelly in the documentary.

King: I'm gonna name the names. Andrea Kelly, your ex-wife, Kitty Jones, Lisa Van Allen, Lizzette Martinez, Jerhonda Pace, Faith Rogers . . .
Kelly: Yeah
King: Asante McGee. You're saying everything they said in that documentary about you is not true.
Kelly: They are lying on me.
King: Why would these women say the same thing about you? That you are controlling, that you are abusive, that you tell women when to eat, when to go to the bathroom, when they can sleep, where they can dress? Why would all these women tell these different stories about you if they were not true? And they don't know each other? That defies logic to me.
Kelly: Right, right, until you hear the explanation. You can start a rumor on a guy like me or a celebrity (snaps fingers) just like that. All you have to do is push a button on your phone and say so-and-so did this to me. R. Kelly did this to me. And if you get any traction from that, if you're

able to write a book from that, if you're able to get a reality show, then any girl that I had a relationship with in the past that it just didn't work out, she can come and say the same exact thing.

King: Are you blaming this on social media?

Kelly: I'm talking about the power of social media!

During this portion of the interview, Kelly attempts to establish and retain the position of truth teller. But as King pushes him on how and why so many people could come forward with consistent accounts, directly questioning Kelly about the validity of the legal charges, the mounting evidence against Kelly becomes more difficult for him to sidestep. Kelly switches tactics, suggesting that those who spoke out against him were motivated by retaliation, greed, and the desire to capitalize on his fame. These tropes are well-established, rhetorical strategies long used to discredit survivors and to perpetuate a cycle of silencing (Tuerkheimer, 2021). The notion that accusers would prey on Kelly because of his wealth, fame, and cultural prominence, using social media to spread rumors and lies, is readily accessible defense to him as a man who already occupies a position of fame and privilege.

At this point, Kelly becomes increasingly, visibly agitated. In the exchange that follows, he is alternately tearful and angry, rising up out of his chair, slapping his fist in his hand, and yelling at King and the camera. Kelly's demeanor during this portion of the interview garnered much attention on social media in the hours and days following its release (*BET*, 2019), in part because his behavior defied the conventions of a celebrity interview in which a star is confronted with serious allegations. Neither repentant nor apologetic, Kelly instead leaned in to his bombastic, hypermasculine image, appearing reactive and belligerent.

Belligerence in broadcast media is a presentational and rhetorical approach that creates a spectacle out of expressions of anger or impatience, intimidation, or exasperation, against an on-screen interlocutor; it may also include manifestations of disgust or frustration (Higgins et al., 2011; Higgins & Smith, 2017). Although expressions of belligerence would normally repel an audience, causing the actor to lose face, in certain circumstances, such as in the accountability interview, the performance of belligerence can represent an effort by the actor to exert power through claims at authenticity and sincerity and depth of expression. Because it appears as a spontaneous, in-the-moment, expression of deeply felt emotion, belligerence seeks to "cu[t] through evasion and obfuscation in the name of immediacy, authenticity, truth and understanding" (Higgins et al., 2011, p. 516). That is to say, belligerence seems to emerge from a place of real and poignant feeling and, as such, may jolt the audience to awareness, creating an impression of rawness as sincerely held feelings rise to the surface and become palpable. Belligerence, therefore, may be interpreted as an authentic expression.

Yet, purposefully belligerent behavior may also take advantage of its association with sincerity; an actor seeking to appear credible and believable may use belligerence as a rhetorical tool. Belligerence can function as a tactic for the reclamation and management of discursive space and an exercise of legitimacy and power through rhetorical might, as the belligerent speaker most often controls the conversation and attracts attention through their outburst (Higgins & Smith, 2017, p. 165). For example, as King's questioning becomes more and more direct, Kelly's response becomes increasingly agitated, and instead of shirking or expressing empathy, he pushes back, forcefully, in a move that allows him to retake control of the interview in a bombastic display.

King: You feel that people have maligned your character?
Kelly: I have been assassinated. I have been buried alive. But I'm alive.
King: So I think the point you're making is, and correct me if I'm wrong, that you have never held anybody against their will.
Kelly: I don't need to. Why would I?
King: You've never held anybody?
Kelly: How stupid would it be for R. Kelly, with all I've been through in my way, way past to hold somebody. Let alone four, five, six, fifty you said? How stupid would I be to do that!
King: I didn't say you were holding
Kelly: That's stupid guys!

Kelly's first rhetorical move towards belligerence can be seen in his repeated use of the word "stupid." As he gradually becomes more upset, raising his voice and speaking in exclamations, Kelly breaks the fourth wall between himself, the camera, and the viewing audience, who are implied by his use of the word "guys." We, the viewers, are now directly implicated in Kelly's outburst, and he uses his apparently righteous anger in an attempt to sway the audience to his position (Higgins & Smith, 2017, p. 166). As the interview continues, Kelly becomes even more irate.

King: I didn't.
Kelly: (*beginning to yell*) Is this camera on me?
King: Yes.
Kelly: (*looking to camera and smacking his fist into his hand*) That's stupid! Use your common sense. Don't. Forget the blogs. Forget how you feel about me. Hate me if you want to. Love me if you want. But just use your common sense. How stupid would it be for me, with my crazy past and what I've been through. Oh right, now I just think I need to be a monster and hold girls against they will. Chain them up in my basement and don't let 'em eat, and don't let 'em out, unless they need some shoes down the street they Uncle!

When Kelly asks King, "Is this camera on me," he points directly behind King, towards the camera, and smacking his fist into his hand, repeats his assertion, "that's stupid!" CBS, in its editorial decision-making, cuts immediately to the camera angle to which Kelly refers. Therefore, when Kelly delivers this line, he is looking straight to camera and directly at the viewers. He speaks the remainder of the above-outlined speech in this way, looking not at King but at his intended audience. His anger here is not *aimed at* the audience but at his accusers; his expression of this anger is instead meant to inculcate the viewer into his rhetorical position, to ignite in his audience a shared sense of indignance (Higgins & Smith, 2017).

Kelly's anger is not, importantly, aimed at his questioner, Gayle King. Indeed, a display of yelling and violent behavior directed towards King, a Black woman, would have been counterproductive to Kelly's denials, as that behavior could appear strikingly similar to that of which he is accused. And so the shift that Kelly performs here is one intended to take the attention away from King and towards an invisible but present public. In this way, Kelly disrupts the conventions of the television interview, reclaims his place at the center of the narrative, and deflects his anger onto the viewing audience.

Through this belligerent questioning, Kelly refers, vaguely, to his own travails. His rhetorical ambiguity is noteworthy, because it allows the audience to fill in the blanks in Kelly's narratives with our own assumptions about what he is referring to. Audiences, especially those who have recently viewed the *SRK* docuseries, will recall the past allegations and legal charges against him and his overt sexual lyrics and performances. In this moment of intense confrontation, Kelly points to his history of cultivating a debased persona as a way of creating a rhetorical way out. Why would anyone, his logic suggests, who is known as a hypersexual figure, who has been accused of sex crimes, be "stupid" enough to actually commit those crimes? In a circular logic, Kelly attempts to convince the audience that his history of outrageousness is a defense against any alleged or future misdeeds. It is here that we see Kelly, in real time, attempting to use gaslighting to convince, dramatically utilizing a tool of psychological abuse on the media audience. Yet Kelly's words also leave the door open for another possible interpretation. His reference to his "crazy past" may also call to mind the sexual abuse that Kelly himself allegedly suffered as a child. In this way, Kelly begins to adopt his desired position that of the victim.

By now, Kelly is in a state of visible distress. He is standing, alternating between anger and tears, gesticulating with punching and slapping motions towards King and the camera/viewer.

King: Robert
Kelly: Stop it. Y'all quit playing. Quit playing.
King: Robert

Kelly: I didn't do this stuff. (*now crying*) This is not me! I'm fighting for my f**n life. Y'all killing me with this shit! (*standing now, visibly upset, screaming*). Thirty years of my career!

King: Robert

Kelly: (*pounding chest*) Y'all trying to kill me! You're killing me man! This is not about music! I'm trying to have a relationship with my kids! And I can't do it! Y'all just don't wanna believe the truth! You don't wanna believe it!

Kelly repeatedly describes the interview as a death. First, he says that he has been "assassinated" and "buried alive" by the allegations against him. Then, seemingly in reference to King's questioning, Kelly shouts, "ya'll triyn' to kill me! You're killin' me man!" Kelly's use of present tense in this exclamation can be interpreted as an accusation against King herself, the broader mass media, or members of the viewing audience who doubt him. Kelly is fighting not only for his life as a free man facing the prospect of incarceration but also for a symbolic life. What is implied, for those who have observed Kelly over the past 30 years, is that the allegations against him represent a symbolic death of the artists' inspirational persona. If found guilty, Kelly's inspirational persona will be obliterated, leaving only the stain of his debased reality. King's questioning draws out the allegations against Kelly. Should the public believe these allegations, Kelly's inspirational persona will be destroyed.

Here, King briefly pauses to "give Kelly a moment." This break disrupts Kelly's cries and provides an opportunity for the host to cut away from his belligerent performance, and, in doing so, reclaim the conventional order of the interview. And yet this break, which occurs at the height of Kelly's emotional outburst, also enhances the dramatic effect of his belligerence and provides Kelly the escape hatch that he seeks when confronted with direct and pointed questions about the allegations of his victims. After this brief interlude, the interview resumes.

Kelly: I hope this camera keeps going.

King: No, we're gonna let the camera keep rolling.

Kelly: It's not **true!** It doesn't even make sense. Why would I hold all these women? Their mothers and fathers told me, we're gonna destroy your career. It's real girls out there missing. It's real young girls out there being abducted, being raped, ok? They really are on chains. They really do have chains on their wrists and they can't get out.

King: Robert

Kelly: This is not me.

Once again, Kelly rhetorically separates himself from the allegations against him as a way of staking his claim as a truth teller. To do so, he positions imagined victims, including himself, as more worthy of sympathy than those who have spoken out against him. This not only undercuts the claims of his accusers but also further perpetuates the idea of a second reality, one in which imagined "real" victims exist and in which he is the aggrieved. In the world of "real" victims, Kelly is a sympathetic man, not a monster. This segment echoes the language in the previous clip, where Kelly notes that in the world of his "lying" accusers, he is the devil. This narrative rests on the construction of and belief in an alternative world. He punctuates this point when he says, "this is not me," a statement that draws on the idea that Kelly's "true" self is distinct from the narratives that are circulating about him. Kelly seeks to bring the audience into his alternative reality, but to succeed, he must convince us to disregard our knowledge of the evidence against him.

Intersectionality and Disbelief

One especially disturbing facet of the way in which Kelly attempts to paint his victims as "unreal" is that his rhetoric supports exiting cultural discourses in which Black women and girls are always already constructed as invisible and unacknowledged victims. Because while many girls and women who speak the truth of their experiences as survivors of sexual assault are not believed, Black girls and women face a disproportionate credibility gap. As legal scholar Deborah Tuerkheimer writes, the intersection between gender and race further disadvantages survivors, and young women of color face especially steep challenges. Among the population most vulnerable to rape, young women ages 18 to 24, less than a third complain to police. Women of color report at even lower rates (Tuerkheimer, 2021, p. 28). This may be, at least in part, because they doubt they will be believed, and they are not wrong to harbor such concerns. Research suggests that prosecutors are less likely to file rape and sexual assault charges due to complaints made by Black accusers and that jurors are more likely to believe similar claims of rape made by White victims (Kennedy, 2003). And prosecutors, aware of this credibility gap, may decline to pursue claims of rape and sexual assault, particularly when they involve Black women and girls, for fear their litigation will fail to result in a conviction (Kennedy, 2003).

Therefore, when it comes to cases to sexual assault and rape, systemic biases disproportionately impact those who may already be most vulnerable or least empowered by existing institutional and cultural structures. Survivors' intersectional identities, including age, race, able-bodiedness, economic status, and sexual orientation, affect the way in which they may experience trauma. The term *intersectionality*, as defined by Kimberlé Crenshaw (1989), encapsulates the "multidimensionality" of experience, as shaped by the interplay of our identities and the ways our identities situate us within a culture. Our identities are shaped by features such as gender and race which, when combined, create new categories whose circumstances and operation within the culture function in new ways (Crenshaw, 1989). When considering R. Kelly's history of abuse, it is crucial to understand that his victims' intersectional identities – as young women and girls of color – meant that they faced specific hurdles when seeking emotional, legal, and community support.

During the first episode of the *SRK* documentary, Mikki Kendall, writer and co-founder of *Hoodfeminism*, discusses the sense of disbelief that Kelly's abuses could have continued over such an extended people of time. "People will say," Kendall explains, " 'well, why didn't anyone notice [that he was pursuing underage girls]?" The answer is that we all noticed; no one cared because we were Black girls" (hampton, 2019, Episode 1). How could this be? The answer lies in the disbelief that Black women and girls face when speaking up. Whether intentional or not, Kelly's choice to prey upon young, Black victims tragically supported his ability to abuse.

In her book *Mediated Misogynoir: Erasing Black Women and Girls' Innocence in the Public Imagination* (2022), scholar Kalima Young echoes Kendall's assertions, writing that the intersection of anti-Blackness and misogyny combined to form a unique hatred of Black women called *misogynoir*, a term developed by Moya Bailey and Trudy (2018) in their study of the role of misogyny in hip hop. Young goes on to outline four tenets of misogyny and racism that support the assertion that a lack of care was shown to Kelly's victims:

> The first is the historical legacy of hypersexuality and sexual violence in Black women and girls' lives. The second is the invisibilization of Black women and girls in anti-rape rhetoric. The third issue is the tendency to place Black women's and girls' liberation secondary to Black men's victimhood status. The final fact is the very real power of the entertainment industry which uses media culture and spectacle to profit from harming Black women and girls.
>
> (Young, 2022, p. 103)

Consider each of these factors in turn. First, the historical, racist legacy of hypersexuality and sexual violence attached to Black women and girls can be traced to slavery and to the commodification and abuse of the Black female body. Discourses about Black women's alleged promiscuity take form in the cultural imagination through the stereotypes of the Jezebel and "Hottentot Venus," which depicted Black women as sexually available and wily. The narratives underpinning such racist tropes are reflected in the biases of the judicial system and the ways rape laws have been adjudicated and enforced. Crenshaw, for example, describes how rape laws were created with the intent to preserve White female chastity. Black men accused of assaulting White women faced harsh penalties, while White men accused by Black women would commonly go unpunished (Leung & Williams, 2019).

Next, the invisibilization of Black women and girls in anti-rape rhetoric can also be observed in contemporary culture. Tuerkheimer writes that White women who come forward with allegations against Black men may actually benefit from a credibility boost, which draws on a history of racist stereotypes concerning the supposed sexual aggression of Black men. Black women who speak out against Black men, however, do not benefit in this way (Tuerkheimer, 2021, p. 15). Young argues that one of the reasons for this is because Black women and, especially, girls are not afforded the same presumption of innocence that White women have enjoyed in American culture. Black girls, Young writes, are "adultified" within our culture, a phenomenon with roots in the history of colonization and enslavement where Black children were viewed as "both disposable and overtly sexual" (2022, p. 13). The intersectional twinning of sexism and racism means that Black girls do not enjoy an assumption of innocence, even in their youth. And this can lead to lack of awareness, allocation of resources, and victim-blaming.

The history of violence against Black women is also inextricably tied to that of their male counterparts. Stereotypes suggesting Black men are angry, violent, oversexed, bestial, and criminal are parallel branches that stem from the same legacy of racism faced by women, and these representations persist in film, television, music videos, and news outlets (Young, 2022, p. 5). Black men also continue to be disenfranchised within American culture, facing higher rates of incarceration, persistent gaps in employment opportunity, and lower rates of economic mobility when compared to White peers (Center for American Progress, 2022). Pew Research Center reports that the Black imprisonment rate at the end of 2018 was nearly twice the rate among Hispanics (797 per 100,000) and more than five times the rate among Whites (268 per 100,000) (Gramlich, 2020). Paradoxically, the embodiment of negative stereotypes around Black masculinity has, at times, helped Black men overcome these systemic inequalities and achieve mainstream success. Hip hop, for instance, as a musical genre has been a field in which Black stars have thrived, and yet it has been criticized for its promotion of hypermasculinity, glorification of violence, and misogynistic treatment of women (Weitzer & Kubrin, 2009).

So when a Black man achieves wealth and prominence – in music, politics, sports, or business – he may represent a sense of hope for other Black people. As writer and cultural critic Jamilah Lemieux explains in *SRK*, R. Kelly's fame and commercial success were sources of pride around his hometown of Chicago and across the country, and he cultivated this in his construction of an inspirational persona. When allegations against him surfaced, they were met with "a knee-jerk instinct to protect him from 'the system,' from the hand of the law, from all these forces that are at play to make sure that Black people, Black men in particular, don't succeed," despite the fact that his crimes were against Black women and girls (hampton, 2019, Episode 3). Thus, the credibility of Kelly's survivors was in tension with Black people's real and important desire to break from deeply ingrained and damaging stereotypes of Black men. "Black female sexual politics," as Young writes, "must always balance the fight against perceptions of Black hypersexuality and the very complex, often messy reality of Black women's sexual lives" (Young, 2022, p. 10).

Finally, the media and entertainment industry continue to profit from the subjugation of Black women and girls. Research shows that Rap and Hip-Hop lyrics often describe women as subordinate, sexual objects who are treated in demeaning ways (Ling & Dipolog-Ubanan, 2017). The pornography industry, valued at about $1.1 billion in 2023 (Ceci, 2023), continues to depict Black women as the subjects of aggression at higher rates when compared to White women, and Black men are more often depicted as aggressors, especially when interacting with Black women (Fritz et al., 2021). And while the entertainment industry has recently faced a reckoning, as a growing number of celebrity women publicly recount their own experiences with coercion, assault, and rape, feminist gains do not often immediately benefit women of color, who continue to be revictimized, shunned, and blamed in the media (Leung & Williams, 2019).

The Limits of Discursive Self-Cleaving

Returning to the close of the CBS interview, Kelly continues to activate and perpetuate the invisibility of girls and women of color as he works to diminish the attention on his victims in favor of his own claims on victimhood.

King: Robert we have to have a conversation. I don't want you just ranting at the camera.

Kelly: I came here for them to hear me talk.

King: Ok.

Kelly: I need help.

King: What kind of help?

Kelly: This is the kind of help I need.

King: Yes. What kind of help?

Kelly: I need somebody to help me not have a big heart. Because my heart is so big, people betray me. (smacking fist) And I keep forgiving them!

King: You sound like you're playing the victim here. You sound like, R Kelly, you do. I listen to you

Kelly: I'm just telling the truth.

King: You're playing the victim card.

Kelly: I'm just telling the truth

King: But Robert

Kelly: And the reason I'm emotional, and I apologize for that

King: No, no no, no

Kelly: is because this the first time I was able to say

King: to speak

Kelly: something. I've said nothing.

King repeatedly stops Kelly, refusing to follow him down his self-dug rabbit hole, calling him out for "playing the victim card" in the final moments of this segment. Her rejection of his claims at victimhood is especially powerful given her own identity as a Black woman. King's reclamation of authority in the final moments of the interview tempers Kelly's outburst, and his closing words ring hollow. Public reaction in the days following the interview airing suggests that Kelly had failed in his attempts to sway viewers. Just as an expression of authenticity is not effective if it is perceived as contrived, so it is also the case when it comes to expressions of belligerence. Many audiences and critics understood Kelly's outbursts as a sympathy ploy, crafted eruptions rather than genuine expressions of exasperation. *Pitchfork* reported that Kelly's mix of rage, anguish, and nonchalance could be understood as a common manipulative strategy employed by abusers (Moreland, 2019).

King's role in holding Kelly accountable represents one of the many links in a chain of action led by women of color who stood up and spoke out, even when facing great personal risk, to draw attention to Kelly's crimes. To understand why it is that Kelly's attempts to self-cleave ultimately failed, we must consider these linkages. Because Kelly did, in fact, successfully use this strategy for many years, maintaining his professional reputation and access to abuse young women and girls. Yet, unlike the other two men profiled in this book, Kelly has now faced a serious legal and public relations reckoning. While it is true that the scope, volume, and nature of Kelly's crimes were excessive and long-standing, thus making the possibility of their discovery and subsequent consequences increasingly probable, it is also important to note that less than 1% of rapes and attempted rapes in the United States result in a felony conviction (Van Dam, 2018), and so the likelihood that Kelly could continue to offend while also enjoying the spoils of fame was quite high. How, then, can we understand why it is that Kelly was ultimately held accountable? And, relatedly, in what contexts might the power and effectiveness of discursive self-cleaving break down?

For decades, Black women and girls had been at the vanguard of efforts to bring attention to Kelly's abuses. In 1996, a high school student named Tiffany Hawkins sued Kelly, alleging that he had sex with her when she was 15 and he was 24; Kelly settled the lawsuit for a quarter of a million dollars (DeRogatis & Pallasch, 2000). In 2001, Tracy Sampson, a former intern at Epic Records, also sued for inappropriate relations and settled for the same sum (Arkin, 2021). Four years later, Kelly's then-wife, Andrea, filed for an order of protection, accusing him of physically assaulting her when she asked for a divorce (Arkin, 2021). As the allegations against Kelly continued to mount, Black women activists, led by Kenyette Barnes and Oronike Odeleye, were working to draw attention to R. Kelly's crimes. In 2017, they began using the hashtag #MuteRKelly to encourage a public reckoning across social media. Protesters petitioned local radio stations in Atlanta, Georgia, where Kelly was allegedly operating a sex cult, to stop playing his music; they also worked to prevent Kelly from performing and protested at his concerts (Leung & Williams, 2019).

#MuteRKelly drew upon and extended the work of activists that had been taking place for more than a decade but was, at that precise moment, reaching the peak of its cultural and political impact. In 2006, it was a Black female activist, Tarana Burke, who founded the #MeToo movement as a social call intended to aid and support women of color in underprivileged communities who had experienced sexual assault. The rising power of #MeToo, combined with the work of Black women activists specifically targeted at Kelly, would ultimately help bring about his indictment. And it was the release of the *Surviving R. Kelly* documentary, produced by, and spotlighting the accounts of, women of color, that finally broke down Kelly's protective armor. Shortly after its release, Sony dropped Kelly from the label and legal charges were brought against him (Cush, 2019).

Surviving R Kelly made public and visible the women whom Kelly had violated. It also presented a raw and unflinching account of the traumatic effects of Kelly's crimes. In doing so, it served as a catalyst for legal action and public outcry that had not, to that point, been forthcoming. *SRK* achieved this by showing Kelly's victims as human beings, women whose lives were irrevocably altered by his abuses. Their emotions, expressions, tears, and body language allowed the audience to understand the depths of Kelly's crimes and to see Black women as worthy of compassion and justice (Leung & William, 2019, p. 366).

It is notable that Kelly's belligerence during the CBS interview was sparked by King's questioning about the *SRK* series and the words of the women who spoke out it. Kelly's reaction underscores his understanding of the fact that it was these women's bravery and the media attention afforded to their words that brought about his downfall. Kelly's attempts to render these women "unreal" throughout the interview, to cast them as less worthy of our attention than "real women," was his way of trying to push his victims back into a place of invisibility. Thankfully, Kelly was not successful in his efforts, and yet the fact that it took so many years, so much suffering, and such sustained protest to finally bring Kelly to justice suggests that there is much more work to be done to ensure that Black women and girls do not continue to face the cycle of silencing that these survivors endured.

The Aftermath

Following its release, *Saturday Night Live* quickly parodied the CBS interview, pointing out Kelly's strategy for laughs. Throughout the opening skit, Keenan Thompson, who played R. Kelly, repeatedly instructs Leslie Jones, who played Gayle King, to call him "victim." This joke makes plain not only the way in which Kelly sought to use the interview to cast himself as the injured party, but also his willingness to play with identity through his self-styled modes of address. The sketch also poked fun at Kelly's defensive logic, with Thompson asking,

> How stupid would it be for me, R. Kelly, with all the crazy legal things that I've done in my past. On tape. And gotten away with. Scott free. To do it again? How stupid do you think I am? . . . Why would I do these things for 30 years? I gave y'all *Trapped in the closet, Feeling on your booty, Age ain't nothing but a number*, and so many other clues!

And in perhaps its most cutting moment, Thompson explained to Jones how easy it is to start a rumor about a celebrity: "All you gotta do is push a button on your phone and say, 'R. Kelly did this to me.' And then attach a video of me doing that thing, and people will believe you! It's scary." The *SNL* sketch revealed Kelly's manipulations and the conflicting nature of the dual roles that he attempted to play in the interview, and in the public sphere more broadly. In doing so, the comedy made obvious, and therefore laughable, both Kelly's defense and the logic of discursive self-cleaving on which it rests. Here we see that Kelly's attempts to weaponize belligerence in service of his appeals have failed to convince, because his performance was not read as sincere but as a contrivance designed to save face.

Yet while the *SNL* skit made light of the obviousness of Kelly's crimes, we should remember that Kelly's abuses were not always so clear. For more than a decade, Kelly managed to engage in a pattern of criminal behavior aided by the entertainment industries, his fans, and his cultivation of contrasting inspirational and debased personas. It was only the collective will of Black women to bring the reality of Kelly's actions into the public eye that ultimately led to his fall. We see, therefore, the critical importance of centering the voices of survivors, particularly those whose intersectional identities have tended to render them invisible, unworthy of victimhood, or otherwise uncredible. We also see the role that media – especially journalism and social media – can play in amplifying and making space for those voices to support and further their impact, and in calling out self-cleaving rhetoric by way of making its machinations visible and ludicrous.

Can public discourse, then, be understood as a capable tool for dismantling the rhetorical strategies of abusers who employ discursive self-cleaving? In some ways, it can. And yet R. Kelly continues to engage in self-cleaving techniques, and some supporters continue to accept this rhetoric, even as he serves times for the crimes of which he has been convicted. In 2022, while in prison, Kelly released an album titled *I Admit It*, in which he continues, to borrow the words of author Nelson George, "to tell on himself" through his lyrics, singing:

> I admit it, I did, did it . . .
> I done f*cked with a couple of fans (fans). . .

I admit I f*ck with all the ladies, that's both older and young ladies (ladies, yeah)
But tell me how they call it pedophile because that shit is crazy (crazy)...
What's the definition of a cult?
What's the definition of a sex slave?...
Look I'm just a man y'all (man y'all)/ Not a monster or beast (no, no)

Predictably, Kelly denied that he dropped the album and made statements to call its reality into question, claiming that the voice in the songs was not his. "I hope people recognized my voice and know that [I] wouldn't be recording in the middle of a legal battle," he told *TMZ* (Madarang, 2022). But while the album would be removed from streaming services, *I Admit It* persists as a media artifact which epitomizes R. Kelly's use of his music as a tool for cultivating his dual persona, one that toys with the concept of reality. Again, he flagrantly admits his crimes but then calls on the public to doubt that he would be foolish enough to blatantly expose his debased persona in this way.

While Kelly's outrageous denial of fact may have lost its effectiveness for some, particularly now that he is in prison, others remain faithful fans, refusing to believe the allegations against him or to stop playing his songs. Some of Kelly's supporters, many of whom are Black women themselves, continued to rally behind him during his trials and even now that he had been convicted. And as Shamira Ibrahim wrote in her reporting for *The Cut*, these supporters are not fringe fanatics but rather ordinary people who find it difficult to give up their fandom, or to accept that a successful Black man is being punished for his sexuality, or to see an exemplar of Black excellence brought low. "We have convinced ourselves," Ibrahim writes, "that there is a social stigma against abusers and predators and those who enable them, yet the celebrity repeatedly proves otherwise" (2021). Ibrahim's reporting echoes the words of #MuteR-Kelly co-founder Tisha Barnes, who explained to *Buzzfeed*, in 2018, that the Black community, and society more broadly, protects problematic Black men who are accused of serious offenses (DeRogatis, 2018). One need only think of the allegations against O.J. Simpson, or Michael Jackson, or Bill Cosby to see that this is the case, particularly when those men enjoy positions of significant wealth and cultural influence.

As audiences, we find it difficult to separate the uplifting, entertaining, and inspiring work of celebrities from what, at times, may be their real and heinous actions. This may be especially so when it comes to figures who have, at some point, symbolically realized a positive step forward in media representation of historically marginalized and silenced groups. To the extent that discursive self-cleaving allows us to compartmentalize our understanding of such public figures, it provides us relief from the cogitative dissonance with which we may be painfully confronted should we accept the apparently contradictory reality. To preserve our fond associations, we may tune out any evidence that disrupts our positive narrative. Yet when we do so, the goals of self-cleaving have been achieved and we become complicit in the cycle of abuse that this rhetoric seeks to conceal.

Note

1 Portions of the CBS interview of R. Kelly, conducted by Gayle King, aired on the network during the first week of March 2019. CBS then released *The Gayle King Interview with R. Kelly*, an hour-long, primetime special, on Friday, March 8, 2019, at 8:00 p.m. (Kiefer, 2019). This was Kelly's first media interview since he was charged with sexually abusing four women, three of them underage, and the meeting between Gayle and Kelly was reported to have lasted 80 minutes (CBS, 2019; Harris, 2019). I accessed and transcribed all portions of the interview quoted in this document using the CBS News YouTube channel. All quotations are transcriptions that I created using the audio in the clips and did not rely on the closed captions provided by the network. I present these exchanges roughly in the order that they occurred throughout the interview; however, because the interview was previously edited by CBS and is not currently available in its 80-minute entirety, these transcriptions do not represent a complete or unedited version of the meeting between Kelly and King. Nevertheless, it is important to note that this segment-style presentation would have been typical of the content viewed by contemporaneous audiences, as CBS aired the interview in portions and these moments circulated, often via short clips, on social media at the time.

References

Arkin, D. (2021, September 27). Timeline of the R. Kelly allegations. *NBC News*.

Bailey, M., & Trudy. (2018). On misogynoir: Citation, erasure, and plagiarism. *Feminist Media Studies, 18*(4), 762–768.

BET. (2019, March 8). *Twitter reacts to R. Kelly's explosive interview with Gayle King*. Retrieved September 16, 2023, from https://www.bet.com/article/jye91s/twitter-reacts-to-r-kelly-s-explosive-interview

Billboard, R. Kelly. Retrieved May 10, 2023, from https://www.billboard.com/artist/r-kelly/

Breihan, T. (2022, March 2). *The number ones: R. Kelly's "Bump N' Grind"*. Stereogum.

CBS. (2019, March 8). *"The Gayle King Interview with R. Kelly": How to watch on TV and online*. Retrieved January 10, 2024, from https://www.cbsnews.com/news/r-kelly-interview-watch-gayle-king-interview-with-r-kelly-cbs-online-live-stream-without-cable-tv-channel-start-time-2019-03-08/

Ceci, L. (2023, March 17). Market size of the online pornographic and adult content industry in the United States from 2018 to 2023. *Statista*.

Center for American Progress. (2022, March 28). *Black Men and the U.S. economy: How the economic recovery is perpetuating systemic racism.* https://www.americanprogress.org/article/black-men-and-the-u-s-economy-how-the-economic-recovery-is-perpetuating-systemic-racism/

Centers for Disease Control and Prevention. (2022, October 11). *Fast facts: Preventing intimate partner violence.* Retrieved May 9, 2023, from https://www.cdc.gov/violenceprevention/intimatepartnerviolence/fastfact.html

Crenshaw, K. (1989). Demarginalizing the intersection of race and sex: A Black feminist critique of antidiscrimination doctrine, feminist theory and antiracist politics. *University of Chicago Legal Forum, 108*, Article 8.

Cush, A. (2019, October 2). R. Kelly's alleged sexual misconduct: A complete timeline. *Spin.*

DeRogatis, J. (2018, March 13). The woman who said R. Kelly abused her refuses to be silenced. *Buzzfeed.*

DeRogatis, J., & Pallasch, A. (2000, December 21). R. Kelly accused of sex with teenage girls. *Chicago Sun Times.*

Fritz, N., Malic, V., Paul, B., & Zhou, Y. (2021). Worse than objects: The depiction of Black women and men and their sexual relationship in pornography. *Gender Issues, 38*, 100–120.

Goffman, E. (1956). *The presentation of self in everyday life.* Anchor Books.

Grady, C. (2021, August 30). 20 years after Aaliyah's death, her story only feels more tragic. *Vox.*

Gramlich, J. (2020, May 6). *Black imprisonment rate in the U.S. has fallen by a third since 2006.* Pew Research.

hampton, D. (2019). *Surviving R. Kelly.* Lifetime.

Haring, B. (2019, March 9). Friday ratings: Gayle King's R. Kelly interview is the night's upset winner. *Deadline.*

Harris, E. A. (2019, March 8). How Gayle King kept her cool in the R. Kelly interview. *The New York Times.*

Heath, C. (2016, February 3). Why R. Kelly calls himself "the pied piper of R&B". *GQ.*

Higgins, M., Montgomery, M., Smith, A., & Tolson, A. (2011). Belligerent broadcasting and makeover television: Professional incivility in Ramsay's *Kitchen Nightmares. International Journal of Cultural Studies, 15*(5), 501–518.

Higgins, M., & Smith, A. (2017). *Belligerent broadcasting: Synthetic argument in broadcast talk.* Routledge.

Hong, N. (2019, December 5). R. Kelly used bribe to marry Aaliyah when she was 15, charges say. *New York Times.*

Ibrahim, S. (2021, September 30). What I learned about R. Kelly's biggest fans. *The Cut.*

Kennedy, E. (2003). *Victim race and rape: A review of recent research.* Brandeis Feminist Sexual Ethics Project.

Kiefer, H. (2019, March 6). Gayle King's R. Kelly interview to be released as hour-long prime-time special by CBS. *Vulture.*

Leung, R., & Williams, R. (2019). #MeToo and intersectionality: An examination of the #MeToo movement through the R. Kelly scandal. *Journal of Communication Inquiry, 43*(4), 349–371.

Ling, J. Q. K., & Dipolog-Ubanan, G. F. (2017). Misogyny in the lyrics of Billboard's top rap airplay artists. *International Journal of Arts Humanities and Social Science*, *2*(6), 7–13.

Madarang, C. (2022, December 10). R. Kelly denies releasing "I admit it" album. *Rolling Stone.*

Moreland, Q. (2019, March 8). How R. Kelly's Gayle King interview shows typical abuser behavior. *Pitchfork.* Retrieved December 9, 2023, from https://pitchfork.com/thepitch/how-r-kellys-gayle-king-interview-shows-typical-abuser-behavior/#:~:text=Kelly%E2%80%9D%20brought%20a%20wider%20consciousness,stops%20to%20assert%20his%20innocence

National Domestic Violence Hotline. (2023). *What is gaslighting?* Retrieved May 9, 2023, from https://www.thehotline.org/resources/what-is-gaslighting/

Petridis, A. (2007, August 20). How did R. Kelly create the world's strangest soap opera? *The Guardian.*

Rietdijk, N. (2021). Post-truth politics and collective gaslighting. *Episteme*, 1–17.

Sammee Ali, S. (2022, September 14). R. Kelly found guilty on 6 counts of child pornography in federal trial. *NBC News.*

Savage, M. (2023, February 24). R. Kelly: The history of his crimes and allegations against him. *BBC.*

Tsioulcas, A. (2021, August 15). Opinion: 13 years after the last R. Kelly Trial, the culture has changed. *NPR.*

Tuerkheimer, D. (2021). *Credible: Why we doubt accusers and protect abusers.* Harper Collins.

Van Dam, A. (2018, October 6). Less than 1% of rapes lead to felony convictions. *The Washington Post.*

Weitzer, R., & Kubrin, C. E. (2009). Misogyny in rap music: A content analysis of prevalence and meanings. *Men & Masculinities*, *12*(1), 3–29.

Young, K. (2022). *Media Misogynoir: Erasing Black women and girls 'innocence in the public imagination.* Lexington Books.

Conclusion

"Judging credibility is," as Deborah Tuerkheimer writes, "a mighty power – because credibility itself is a form of power" (2021, p. 3). So, too, is our ability to call out that which is incredible, to mark it as unbelievable, evasive, or deceptive. When we allow ourselves, individually and as a society, to be persuaded, despite our better judgment, by those who would seek to convince us to their side using self-cleaving strategies, we forfeit that power. Over the past five years, as #MeToo and other activists and organizations have worked to reframe victim-survivors as believable narrators of their own lived experiences, the question of whose stories are told, heard, and believed is a critical terrain on which a struggle over the power of credibility has been fought. At the start of the #MeToo movement, it seemed that a public reckoning was underway, a seismic shift towards women which, many promised, would never yield back to the misogynistic silencing of yesteryear.

But power does not shift so easily or permanently in one direction. As Susan Faludi reminds us, when women achieve material gains in their rights, finances, and freedom, they often face an insidious counterassault that seeks to slow, and even reverse, those gains (Faludi, 1991). "We will find such flare-ups," Faludi writes, "are hardly random; they have always been triggered by the perception – accurate or not – that women are making great strides" (1991/2006, p. 10). It is when women are closest to achieving progress that backlash emerges to shut it down. Now this is not to say that there is some great conspiracy designed to achieve this, no coordinated organization. Backlash is subtle, diffuse, and dynamic (Faludi, 1991/2006, p. 13). But it is this very subtlety that makes it all the more pernicious, even harder to see, and prompts us to wonder if it isn't all in our own heads (Faludi, 1991/2006, pp. 13–14). By appearing not to be political, to be simple celebrity gossip, the tawdry and not-unexpected bad behavior of the wealthy and famous, discursive self-cleaving functions as a form of political backlash that may easily go unnoticed as such.

Already, we see counterattacks aimed at those who speak out against famous men, even in the face of detailed and compelling evidence, even when those men have been found guilty by the legal system. Some argue that we should not be so quick to "cancel" these men, to try to remove them – along with their

DOI: 10.4324/9781003380139-5

words, their films, their music – from the public sphere. The cultural greatness of men is often used as a defensive rationale (Dederer, 2017). We should all, this logic goes, be able to separate the artist from the art, a lifetime of achievements from a few (or a dozen) so-called mistakes. This is an argument that foregrounds the power and prominence of perpetrators at the expense not only of victims but of public morality and of the rights of women more broadly. As such, it is a logic that reaffirms and seeks to shore up predatory masculinity and a misogynistic social order.

Still, we have seen moments in which this logic has been successfully challenged. When it comes to men who have used self-cleaving discourse as an image management strategy, there have been times when this rhetoric has ultimately failed to guard them against the consequences of their actions, where the interlocking institutional protections, legal strategies, and efforts to sway media sentiment have proven ineffective (Greer & McLaughlin, 2021). These instances, as Greer and McLaughlin (2021) make clear in their research on the English serial pedophile Jimmy Savile, often occur when structural protections and modes of social privilege have diminished to a point where the mask of the abuser can be pulled away and a new, critical narrative can take hold in the public consciousness. It is this opportunity for revelation that serves as a tipping point, one that can prompt a new wave of media scrutiny and criminal investigation. And so we may ask, under what circumstances does self-cleaving fail?

As this book has attempted to show, fame is a primary institutional protection on which self-cleaving relies. The greater the degree of fame enjoyed, the greater the degree of protection, and vice versa. So lack of renown, or waning celebrity, may prevent an individual from reaping the benefits of self-cleaving (Boyle, 2019, p. 113). In the first instance, we can consider the case of Brock Turner, a Stanford student accused of raping and assaulting a woman at a fraternity party. At trial, Turner, whose case was covered extensively across national media but who was not widely known prior to his arrest, attempted to rhetorically construct multiple subjectivities, invoking a fractured self-subject in his account of his attack to minimize his responsibility, yet he was ultimately found guilty (Brand, 2022). In the second case, we can consider someone like Bill Cosby, who, by the time he faced a legal reckoning for decades of alleged abuses, was an aging man, no longer the star of one of America's most popular sitcoms, and finally unable to use his public image to effectively conceal his crimes.

In other cases, including Cosby's, there may come a point in which the volume and severity of allegations become so overwhelming that public sentiment finally turns (Boyle, 2019). Importantly, it is often the work of women who step forward at great personal risk, insisting that these individuals are brought to justice, who push the evidence into the public sphere and prompt such revelations. Here, we can consider again the role of dream hampton's documentary, the survivors who appeared in it, and the women who created the campaign to

#MuteRKelly, whose collective efforts sparked public realization, leading to criminal charges.

It is also of note that the degree to which an actor conforms to an idealized, hegemonically masculine persona is a crucial factor in determining his ability to successfully deploy self-cleaving strategies. The more physically attractive, socially dominant, and financially powerful, the less likely he is to lose public support (Boyle, 2005). The intersection of race and sexuality plays an important role, as it is White, heterosexual, wealthy men who benefit most from credibility inflation (Tuerkheimer, 2021). Men who are overweight, aging, or perceived as weak are less likely to compel public trust (Boyle, 2019). And Black men, including Bill Cosby and R. Kelly, are some of the few who have faced a legal reckoning for their crimes and have served time in prison. This point once more draws our attention to the ways in which race, particularly Blackness, is situated within the structures of power that shape perceived credibility. While Black women and girls may be less likely to be believed than Black men, Black men are less likely to be believed than White men. As we have seen in the case of R. Kelly, this dynamic functioned in ways that disenfranchised Kelly's victims, while simultaneously reinforcing perceptions of injustice among Black fans who understood Kelly's conviction as racially motivated (Young, 2022).

The final circumstance which may lead to the breakdown of self-cleaving occurs when the celebrity dies. In death, the power of the star to compel us with their image and to maintain one or more convincing public masks is eroded. As audiences, we may feel a greater psychological distance from celebrities once they are no longer alive, and this allows us to examine their legacy in a more critical fashion (Paasonen & Horeck, 2023). Yet a cultural reliance on this eventuality as a form of justice is ultimately insufficient because it does nothing to challenge abuse as it happens, nor to upset existing structures of power that allow such violence to continue. It is far easier, even pat, to accept a person's history of violence in retrospect, because such an acknowledgment requires little of us. We may choose not to watch a certain film or listen to a certain album and our sentiments towards that figure may shift, but our ability to consider ourselves good and moral persons is not fundamentally disrupted. We can comfort ourselves, even if we held suspicions, that we never really knew, and so what could we possibly have done at the time?

What Can Be Done?

But what *can* we do, in our own ways, to interrupt and challenge the power of self-cleaving? I propose that there are concrete steps media producers and consumers can take to subvert this rhetoric and to prevent it from gaining further momentum in our public discourse.

First, journalists should refrain from referring to alleged abusers in fantastical terms. Calling such individuals *monsters*, *devils*, *demons*, *ghouls*, and *vampires* may seem apt; however, this terminology works to situate sexual misconduct and violence within the realm of the fantastical and unreal (Andreasen, 2023; Mack & McCann, 2021). When media narratives report transgressions in ways that evoke such shapeshifters, the public's understanding of the distinction between reality and fantasy is further weakened (Durham, 2022, p. 18). This language therefore supports the attempts of abusers seeking to inhabit an ambiguous dreamland where reality is uncertain and personas may be split and multiple. An emphasis on monstrous masculinity also positions male violence as abhorrent, extreme, and other and, in doing so, obfuscates the ways in which criminal and abusive behavior is connected to so-called *typical* male behavior and hegemonic masculinity more broadly (Boyle, 2019, p. 118). That is to say, when we "other" abusers, casting them out as deviant and distinct, we ignore the many ways in which their actions have been enabled, even encouraged, by intersecting cultural, political, and institutional forces. To render abusers, and survivors, more visible, it is important that we understand perpetrators not as monsters, though their actions may certainly be horrific, but as human beings whose behaviors reflect and contribute to toxic expressions of gendered and raced power that are all too ordinary.

Next, media consumers should not hesitate to call out self-cleaving discourse when we hear it. We should be attuned to instances in which famous figures, especially those accused of sexual misconduct, attempt to occupy multiple subject positions and to deny evidence that is well-documented, compelling, and in the public domain. Further, when we notice such discourse in action, we should not keep our observations to ourselves. We should, to the extent that we feel safe to do so, point this strategy out to our friends, our family members, or on social media. "We must," as Kurt Anderson urges, "call out the dangerously untrue and unreal . . . to adopt new protocols for information-media hygiene" (2017, p. 19). We should not think of this as some petty gossip or frivolous anti-fandom – these are characterizations that so often work to trivialize and thereby dismiss the meanings and values of celebrity culture – but as an act of political resistance.

Government also has a role to play in bringing abusers to justice, particularly given the technological challenges that lie ahead (Wu, 2023). Discursive self-cleaving, as this book has shown, often calls on us to doubt the veracity of mediated information, including video and audio content. As artificial intelligence (AI) makes it easier to create ever-more convincing images, voiceovers, and videos – all fake – these technologies further blur the line between evidence and fiction, offering plausible deniability for those seeking to evade the consequence of their actions. Technology is never neutral and often reinforces existing structures of power, including those around gender, and we have already seen the ways in which A.I. technologies can be deployed to create non-consensual nude images, sexually explicit videos, and other forms of pornography, which are disproportionately aimed at manipulating, objectifying, and consuming the bodies and identities of women and girls (Wagner & Blewer, 2019). Regulation has a role to play in establishing guardrails that help the public to identify content that is, or that may be, generated through A.I., so that we can better make sense of deepfake content and its potential motivations. If government fails to act, confidence in our own ability to interpret media in informed and rational ways is at risk of being further eroded and abusers may find it ever easier to hide in plain sight.

The gains of #MeToo and women's rights movements, both in America and around the globe, are increasingly in jeopardy (Gupta, 2019). Be wary of the claims that we are currently in a post-#MeToo moment. History tells us that political change is never easily won or maintained. Backlash is almost always assured. We should not assuage ourselves with the comforting notion that such abuses would not happen today. They are happening and they will continue to happen. And should abusers be able to persuade us with their narratives, to compel us to turn our thoughts away from that which we have observed with our very eyes, they will have won a significant victory at the expense of victim-survivors who have bravely refused to be silenced. #MeToo has helped tip the scales of credibility ever so slightly in favor of women, and victims of all genders, but if we are not vigilant to the insidious strategies of those in power who seek to do others harm, the hard-fought gains that have been won can easily be lost. The scales can tip back with the slightest touch.

If discursive self-cleaving continues to gain momentum as an effective strategy among famous and powerful men, we risk a number of significant consequences. The most notable risk is to those who have been abused. The successful deployment of self-cleaving rhetoric is inversely tied to the credibility of victim-survivors. The more successfully abusers can convince the public with their rhetoric, the more the credibility of victim-survivors is once again quelled and the potential for psychological re-victimization is heightened. Still, it is not only survivors but all of us who are imperiled by such discourse, for it works to normalize and excuse sexual violence in all forms, thus contributing to a culture where rapacious masculinity is enabled and engrained.

This is also a milieu in which truth loses meaning, in which there is no way of testing the veracity of a matter because we cannot even agree on basic points of fact (Ball, 2017). Reality becomes totally subjective. Manipulative rhetoric distracts, takes precious resources to disprove, and adds to the growing sense that we may as well believe what we want, since it's all subjective anyway (Ball, 2017, p. 1). As the philosopher Alasdair MacIntyre contends, in a world where meaning breaks down, we develop a sense of arbitrariness and debates about morality seem to go on without end because there is no "rational way of securing moral agreement" (1981, p. 6). Here, knowledge itself becomes devalued, as it is no longer the fact of the thing, but one's ability to confidently assert it, that renders its claim and claimant powerful (Higgins, 2018, p. 136).

Nearly 30 years ago, Richard Schickel worried about the ability of celebrities to break down the intellectual and psychological barriers of our perception, and he urged audiences to be wary of those who would seek to blur the lines of image and reality, to playact trust, authenticity, and responsibility to suit their own ends (1986, pp. 363–365). The most dangerous kind of public figures, to Schickel, were those involved in an "inner contradiction of devastating proportions." They cannot be trusted, and will eventually do harm, because "they do not know who they are" (1986, p. 364). And so Schickel urged audiences to "break away from all metaphors, to see our subject steadily and whole" so that we may understand how celebrities' "comfortable evasions" contribute to an alarmingly altered understanding of our contemporary reality (1986, p. 365). Although the past three decades have brought about many changes in the nature and scope of celebrity culture, and technologies have altered our experiences as media consumers, the relevance of Schickel's admonitions persists.

Sexual misconduct, violence, and rape are difficult topics to face. We do not want to imagine that celebrities, especially those whom we find entertaining, whom we have grown to know and feel connected to over many years, could commit such crimes. Self-cleaving rhetoric offers us, the audience, a comfortable out, an opportunity to disbelieve that which we do not want to find credible. But we should not settle for a placid ignorance since, after all, as Frankfurt reminds us, "hiding our eyes from reality will not cause any reduction of its dangers and threats; plus, our chances of dealing successfully with the hazards that it presents will surely be greater if we can bring ourselves to see things straight" (2006, pp. 57–58). Our ability to recognize, call out, and challenge self-cleaving rhetoric is a crucial mobilization of media literacy, an act of gender solidarity with women and girls, and a rejection of the creeping culture of mendacity. Though storytelling is only one tool for generating political will and, ultimately, lasting change, it is an important one. We should be wary of those who use their power to prevent survivors from being heard and believed.

References

Anderson, K. (2017, September). How America lost its mind. *The Atlantic.*

Andreasen, M. B. (2023). A monster, a pervert, and an anti-hero: The discursive construction of Harvey Weinstein, Kevin Spacey, and Louis C.K. in humorous #MeToo memes. *Feminist Media Studies, 23*(5), 2218–2234.

Ball, J. (2017). *Post-truth: How bullshit conquered the world.* Biteback Publishing.

Boyle, K. (2005). *Media and violence: Gendering the debates.* Sage.

Boyle, K. (2019). *#MeToo, Weinstein and feminism.* Palgrave.

Brand, A. (2022). White masculine abjection, victimhood, and disavowal in rape culture: Reconstituting Brock Turner. *Quarterly Journal of Speech, 108*(2), 148–171.

Dederer, C. (2017, November 20). What do we do with the art of monstrous men? *The Paris Review.*

Durham, M. G. (2022). *MeToo: The impact of rape culture in the media.* Polity.

Faludi, S. (2006). *Backlash: The undeclared war against American women* (15th ed.). The River Press. (Original work published 1991)

Frankfurt, H. (2006). *On truth.* Alfred A. Knopf.

Greer, C., & McLaughlin, E. (2021). The celebrity icon mask: The multiinstitutional masking of Jimmy Savile. *Cultural Sociology, 15*(3), 364–385.

Gupta, A. H. (2019, December 4). Across the globe, a "serious backlash against women's rights". *The New York Times.*

Higgins, M. (2018). The Donald: Media, celebrity, authenticity, and accountability. In C. Happer, A. Hoskins, & W. Merrin (Eds.), *Trump's media war* (pp. 129–141). Palgrave.

MacIntyre, A. (1981). *After virtue: A study in moral theory.* University of Notre Dame Press.

Mack, A. N., & McCann, B. J. (2021). "Harvey Weinstein, monster": Antiblackness and the myth of the monstrous rapist. *Communication and Critical/Cultural Studies, 18*(2), 103–120.

Paasonen, S., & Horeck, T. (2023). "Natalie Wood day": Sexual violence and celebrity remembrance in the #MeToo Era. *Celebrity Studies, 14*(4), 534–547.

Schickel, R. (1986). *Intimate strangers: The culture of celebrity.* Fromm International Publishing Corporation.

Tuerkheimer, D. (2021). *Credible: Why we doubt accusers and protect abusers.* Harper Wave.

Wagner, T. L., & Blewer, A. (2019). "The word real is no longer real": Deepfakes, gender, and the challenges of AI-altered video. *Open Information Science, 3*, 32–46.

Wu, T. (2023, November 7). In regulating A.I., we may be doing too much: And too little. *The New York Times.*

Young, K. (2022). *Media Misogynoir: Erasing Black women and girls 'innocence in the public imagination.* Lexington Books.

Index